The Life & Legacy of Lear Green

by
Symoné Miller, MSS, LCSW

Kate,
Thank you for your support.

Symoné Miller

D0813797

ISBN: 978-0-578-57303-8

The Life and Legacy of Lear Green

Proudly self-published through Divine Legacy Publishing, www.divinelegacypublishing.com

Dedication

This book is dedicated to my Godmother, Lear Green, the woman who has loved and supported me as her own since the very beginning. The depth of my love for you, I could never fully show but this book is a slight rendition of how much you have influenced me.

Acknowledgements

This book would not have been possible without God giving me the vision and allowing me to follow through with not only the writing of this book but its publication. I am forever grateful for God using me as a vessel to share my Godmother's story while beginning my healing process.

I could not have written this book without my husband, Timon. You have been my greatest support, pushing me to not only write this book but always reminding me why it is needed and how important it is to me. Thank you for your listening ear, your love, your encouragement, and for being my sounding board throughout this journey.

To my mother, Mary, thank you for always believing in me and for pushing me to strive for greatness. I carry the values you have instilled in me daily and thank you for your many sacrifices.

To my beautiful sister of Sigma Gamma Rho Sorority, Incorporated, Arlene, thank you for your constant check ins and holding me accountable for accomplishing my dreams. Thank you for always being your sister's keeper.

Thank you to my Soror, writing coach, editor and publisher, Amanda Chambers and the entire Divine Legacy Publishing family, for your commitment to me and helping to make my dream a reality.

To my friend Thelma, thank you for holding me down during this past year as I became an author. Your support does not go unnoticed.

Introduction

At the end of 2018, my godmother had a health scare at 95 years old, and it was recommended that she have surgery to address her irregular heart rate. It was then when I realized that she would not live forever, which took a while for my heart to accept although my mind already knew this to be true. It was at that point that I decided to begin writing my godmother's story down on paper to honor her legacy but also to help me with accepting that she is not immortal and that there will be a day when I can no longer hear her voice or see her face. So, as much as this book will teach and benefit others, it was also written to begin my healing process of the inevitable. I wanted my godmother's story to be passed down to future generations to learn about the woman who has lived through nine decades and has a wealth of history and knowledge to share. There are many famous people who have done many things, but I wanted to let my godmother know that she did not need to lead a march or create an invention to be important and to be remembered in history. This book highlights the struggles and triumphs of my godmother's life from her being raised in poverty, to working under the Jim Crow era, marrying her husband,

and working through the demands and surprises that marriage offers to her present life.

If asked to describe my godmother in one word, I would be utterly speechless because she is kind, nurturing, caring, resourceful, influential, humble, generous, and resilient to have overcome a life of poverty and oppression. This book signifies that against all odds, with faith and perseverance, anything is possible.

Welcome to my labor of love…

Chapter One

In the 1800s, there was a woman of African descent who was a slave owned by a man who inherited her from his mother-in-law. The woman met a free African American man named William Adams and as time progressed they began to court. As the two fell in love, William asked for the woman's hand in marriage. Due to fear of having children born into slavery like herself, the woman was reluctant to accept this invitation to matrimony. William remained persistent in asking for the woman's hand in marriage, resulting in her later agreeing with the idea that she would escape from slavery to enter marriage as a free woman. Although the risk was great, both the woman's mother and William's mother, a free woman, orchestrated a plan for her to escape.

This plan included William's mother, a sailor's chest, and a trip on a ship. The chest was packed with essentials, such as food and water along with the woman hidden inside. William's mother was assigned to the deck of the ship where she was able to keep a close eye on the chest. During the night hours, William's mother would discreetly untie the chest to check on the woman and allow her to get some fresh air. This trip was a long passage that lasted eighteen hours, but it was worth the risk as the taste of freedom was indeed sweet. After arriving in Philadelphia, a state where slavery was nonexistent, William and the woman married and lived together for three years in wedded bliss until the young woman died unexpectedly of unknown causes. This young woman's name was Lear Green. Sixty three years later on a farm in Beaufort, South Carolina, a baby was born who had the same name; this cannot be a coincidence.

On a hot summer day in Beaufort, South Carolina, a baby girl was born to an unwed mother, Flourine Seabrook, and an unknown father. This baby was named Lear and she arrived into the world on August 23, 1923. Shortly after her birth, Lear was given to her maternal grandparents, Julia and Isaac Seabrook, by her mother who was young and wanted to be "free" from the care and responsibility of a child but also wanted her child to be loved and taken care of. As an infant, the elders told Lear's grandparents that she would not live long because she was sick. Looking back at this, Lear did not recall what kind of sickness she reportedly had, if the elders even knew, but she just remembers being told that she could not drink cow's milk as an infant but instead was given goat's milk to sustain her life. Lear's grandparents ignored the comments of the elders and continued to care for her with pride as she was their first grandchild. During those times when a baby would cry, caregivers would put a small amount of sugar in a cloth, tightly twist it up then wet the cloth to give to the baby to suck on. This was done to keep the baby quiet; similar to caregivers giving babies a pacifier in today's society.

Lear's grandmother was small in stature, approximately 5'5", had a thin frame and chocolate skin free from blemishes. When asked about childhood rearing and discipline, Lear stated, "them old folks was strict back in the days." This was taken to mean that in the 1920s, discipline was high as it was important for children to be well-mannered and respectful to their elders. Children did what they were told to do and did not talk back or question adults when given instructions. In today's society, parent's may tell their children when they misbehave to go get the belt for a spanking, but when Lear was in trouble she was told to go get a switch. A switch is a thin piece of tree branch with the leaves removed and this switch was used for spankings. Lear would initially pick a thick switch so that it would be less painful as her grandmother struck her, but her grandmother would instruct Lear to go back out in the field for another switch until it was to her liking. Although Lear did not enjoy these moments, she still held her grandmother in the highest regard because she knew that the spankings were not done to hurt her but to teach her a lesson to do what she was told and expected to do.

Lear describes her childhood as similar to the commercials of people in Africa who walked in dirt roads living in poverty. The family home was built by Lear's grandfather with a large porch on the front and another porch on the side. Once inside the home, there was an attic where family members would sleep when they infrequently came to visit. There was a sense of community in the 1920s, where neighbors would help each other. For example, if someone's home burned down, the entire community would come together to rebuild it.

During this time in history, blacks and whites were not allowed in the same hospital, so a doctor would come to the home to evaluate the person. Once this was done, the doctor would give instructions for the caregiver which included sterilizing the sick person's clothes with lye to prevent spreading the illness to the others in the home. The caregiver would have to use a washboard and rub the clothing back and forth in homemade soap made with lye. This level of resourcefulness was incredible during this time as the caregiver was typically a volunteer who would walk sometimes for miles to care for a person who was ill.

Natural remedies date back for generations and generations and the Beaufort community was no different. They would make medicine for colds, influenza, high blood pressure, and diabetes among other things. Elders would steep pine needles, seaweed and lemon to cure the common cold and influenza. They would also take cherry bark and pine needles to cure whooping cough and common colds. There were teas developed to cleanse a person's body but all of these natural remedies have been intercepted and now if these things are found in a person's home in South Carolina they could go to jail because these things are to be purchased from the store only.

Some of Lear's fondest memories are of cooking in the family home. One tradition in the household was making pie using sweet potatoes. Lear and her grandmother would sit at the kitchen table and grate fresh sweet potatoes. After grating the potatoes, they would mix those raw grated sweet potatoes with eggs, seasonings, canned milk, flavoring, and butter like a batter then cautiously put these mixed ingredients into an iron pan to prepare it for baking. It would bake in the fireplace mantle that resembled a barbecue grill since the family did not have a stove. While baking the pie in the fireplace, wood would be placed in the fireplace to keep the flames low enough to cook the pie but also to prevent the pie from burning. As the pie cooked, the sweet aroma would fill the home and the entire family would patiently wait to cut it. This delectable dish was called "sweet potato poon." Eating meat with meals was seen as a delicacy. The family would cook the fat from the upper part of a pig's side, especially when dried and salted in strips, which was nicknamed fatback. The grease from the fatback would be placed on a plate of grits and eggs with a small piece of the fatback. As Lear would eat dinner, she remembers nibbling on the fatback to savor the flavor as she ate the remainder of the meal.

In the morning, Momma, as Lear affectionately called her grandmother, would tell Lear to go get two chickens for supper. Looking at this request with today's lens one would decipher this as Lear's grandmother making a request for her to go to the store and buy two whole chickens from the supermarket. During that time, the instructions were very literal. Lear was to go into the field, grab a chicken by the neck and wring its neck until it was dead to bring it home for supper. One may find that to be inhumane or dangerous, but that was the way of life in the country and anything else would have been out of the normal routine. Lear's grandfather would make homemade syrup that was used for breakfast. This syrup was made from the juice of the sugar cane.

Lear's mother, Fluorine, did not live in South Carolina, so Lear's visitation with her mother was infrequent as she had to visit her via boat to Savannah,

Georgia. Around 1931, Lear's mother began to take ill resulting in Lear's grandmother bringing her back home so that she could care for her during her time of need. Once Fluorine arrived at the Seabrook home, she was taken to the back bedroom and placed there until her untimely demise. Unfortunately, Lear did not know the cause of her mother's death as medical attention was scarce. The most common causes of death in the 1930s were cancer, influenza, pneumonia, tuberculosis, and heart disease so one may suspect that Fluorine died of one of these illnesses, but there is no way to be certain. Since Lear was not raised by her mother, there was a disconnect when she learned of her mother's death. She reports being sad because death in general was seen as a sad thing but does not describe her mother's death as life altering since they had a distant relationship.

Lear's grandparents could not read or write, which resulted in them signing their names with an X on whatever documentation was presented to them. Therefore the importance of education was not something emphasized to Lear as her grandparents did not know the benefits of getting an education themselves. Lear remembers her grandparents sharing with her that her great grandparents were slaves and that everyone had to do the same work. When the women would get tired and were unable to do their share, the husbands would attempt to help them, resulting in the husbands being beaten to stop them from working together.

Lear completed five years of formal schooling then began "working in the field" to help her grandparents, not realizing the opportunities that would await her if she pursued an education. She remembers sitting in class with her peers playing in her long jet black hair.

This was a magical time for Lear in which her mind would wander and she would fall asleep as her peers would twist her hair.

The Great Depression is characterized as an economic recession that crippled primarily the United States of America's economy beginning in 1929 and lasted for ten years. When Lear was asked about her memories of The Great Depression, there was a brief and awkward silence. She reported that this time did not make an impact on her life because her family was already poor living on the farm where her grandparents raised all their own food including chickens, pigs, bows, peas, corn, black eyed peas, and everything in between. Her family learned to live on the land and make use of all the things the land had to offer. For instance, if the corn that was grown was too hard, it would be ground up by Lear's grandfather into either cornmeal or grits to be used in another capacity. Cornmeal is a flour-like substance with a gritty texture that is commonly used as a breading on foods prior to frying.

Lear also learned to rinse rice thoroughly with water and utilize the water from that rice to make starch to press clothing. Her grandparents earned their income by selling the food from their farm to locals. Their farm was located in close proximity to the river so the family would go to the river and go fishing for all kinds of seafood including but not limited to fish, shrimp, clams, scallops, and crabs all for free. As Lear reflected on this time, she mentioned that nowadays a license is needed to fish in the river. She describes this as just another way for "the man," referring to white people, to have control and make a profit off of something they had for years. Back in the 1930s, families did not pay taxes on their property, therefore they could live off their land

and raise their animals for generations, but this all changed when the government came in and made people pay taxes.

Four years into The Great Depression, President Franklin D. Roosevelt took office as the 32nd President of the United States while in his second term as governor of New York. As President Roosevelt began his presidency term, there were roughly 13 million people unemployed. He worked diligently to restore the public's confidence stating in his first inaugural address, "The only thing we have to fear is fear itself." President Roosevelt promised action and in the mid-1930s he developed The Work Projects Administration (WPA), which was created with the purpose to provide work for millions of people affected by the Great Depression. This program employed primarily men who did not have the skills to complete public projects including building hospitals, storm drains, school buildings, bridges, planting trees, and roadside cleaning. Lear describes President Roosevelt as the first president she actually liked because he allowed jobs for black and white people. Although the Great Depression did not directly have an impact on Lear, a cataclysm occurred throughout the United States of America.

At the age of eighteen, Lear experienced her most devastating loss with the death of her grandmother, Momma. It was at that point, Lear did not believe she could go on and live without her grandmother in her life as she was lost and filled with sadness and despair. Somehow Lear found an inner strength to move on as she knew this was what her grandmother would have ultimately wanted for her.

Chapter Two

Beginning in the 1800s, there was a racial segregation system known as Jim Crow primarily in the southern states. This system was named after a white comedic entertainer who performed as an uneducated slave and later painted his face black while speaking in an accent that he perceived was a slave. The entire Jim Crow system supported the sentiment that whites were superior to blacks in every way imaginable and did not encourage treating blacks as nothing more than second class citizens or even animals in some instances. There were protocols in place to create a social normality for the way blacks would be allowed to interact with whites. These protocols included whites automatically having the right of way at street intersections, interracial marriage and adoptions were prohibited, whites and blacks could not be served in the same dining room, black men could not offer to light the cigarette of a white female as this would imply companionship, and so forth. Blacks could not show any form of affection towards each other while in public as this was offensive to whites.

During the Great Migration, from approximately 1915-1960, more than 6 million African Americans moved from the south to areas in the north such as Chicago, Philadelphia, and New York. This relocation was triggered in an effort to escape the stringent segregation in the south with hopes of financial success and prosperity in the northern states. Blacks were escaping the south to the north to escape the blatant violence and lynching of the Ku Klux Klan and prevent living under the Black Codes. The Black Codes were laws designed to restrict the freedom of blacks in various capacities even after slavery was technically abolished.

Whites would have blacks sign labor contracts under the Black Codes and if they resisted they were fined, arrested, or even forced into unpaid labor much like legal slavery. These Black Codes included civil rights, labor contracts, vagrancy, apprenticeship, court, crimes, and punishments. In South Carolina the black code applied only to people of color, which specifically included anyone with more than one-eighth of Negro blood. Who knows how one can determine if someone has more than one-eighth of Negro blood? During these times, it was said if you had an ounce of black in you, you were considered black so this is the way blacks viewed this code.

Jim Crow laws consistently impacted the lives of African Americans from how they traveled to where they could shop to where and how they could eat their meals. Jim Crow enforced and advocated for segregation of schools, parks, trains, buses, restrooms, and everything in between. The segregation was also shown by labeling these public places with either "Colored" or "Whites Only" leaving no room for confusion. If a black person would enter a place that was for whites only, they could be arrested and placed in jail for breaking the law. The places that were allocated for blacks were subordinate in treatment and the resources were not comparable.

These laws also prohibited blacks from moving into white communities, leaving them to live in often substandard housing or living with relatives while saving money as the price of homes were often out of reach for them. If blacks would try to take a stand against these unjust laws they were putting their lives and the lives of their families at risk including lynchings, losing their jobs, or even burning crosses on the front lawn of their property to evoke fear. These forms of retaliation were not taken seriously by legal enforcement made up of white men who often times were outwardly supportive of segregation.

During the late 1930s to 1940s, housework was defined by Lear as working one steady job in a particular house. On the other hand, days work was defined as cleaning a different house everyday, therefore a woman could go to five homes a week to earn a week's pay to support herself and often times her family.

It was from 1932 to 1972 that there was a study of syphilis in Alabama. The United States Public Health Service worked with the Tuskegee Institute to study syphilis by gathering black male volunteers only, promising them two things: free medical treatment and burial insurance for their participation. In hindsight, one may wonder why burial insurance was offered as an incentive instead of financial compensation. Researchers were dishonest with the male volunteers telling them they were being treated for "bad blood" which was a common term used to describe multiple illnesses from iron deficiency, syphilis, and exhaustion, but this was not the case.

The study consisted of 600 black men, 201 of which did not have syphilis. It was discovered years after the experiment began that the participants of the study did not give informed consent. Informed consent means that each participant of a study must be informed of the purpose of the study, its risks, the possible side effects and the benefits of participating. Not only were the men misinformed about their participation in the study, they were never given the proper treatment for syphilis even when the appropriate treatment, penicillin, became available. Without the proper treatment these men were subject to serious health challenges such as blindness, becoming mentally ill, and even dying as syphilis brutally attacked their bodies.

It was not until the mid 1960s that the experiment was found to be unethical. So for thirty years the United States performed unethical testing while destroying the lives of only black men who were recruited for this experiment. Although this was not a concern to those conducting the experiment, allowing these black men to remain untreated posed serious risks to the black community as a whole including these men passing the sexually transmitted disease to their spouses and their children at birth. This is a prime example of how blacks were seen as inferior and were used for experimentation without any regard for their well-being.

Now as an adult in the 1940s, Lear was officially living independently and working full time cleaning homes. In 1942, while renting a room in Beaufort, Lear met a man named Albert Green who was affectionately nicknamed "Slim Green" by those close to him. Albert received his nickname by being a well dressed man standing over six feet tall with dark chocolate skin and an infectious smile while having a sense of humor and working in construction. Albert was also renting a room on a nearby street that Lear could see from her window. The two began courting shortly after meeting and later became inseparable. Lear introduced Albert to her grandfather in the midst of their courtship as a sign of respect seeing that her grandfather raised her and it was a pleasant experience. As the courting continued, discussions of Lear and Albert moving in together surfaced. Lear stood firm with her decision not to move into a home with Albert prior to being married so after a year of dating, Lear and Albert decided to officially tie the knot.

One humid summer morning on Albert's birthday, Saturday August 28th, 1943, Lear and Albert dressed in their Sunday's best clothing. Lear, in a black knee-length sleeveless dress, and Albert, in a well-tailored suit, headed to the courthouse to get married with Albert's five year old niece trailing along. Albert's niece was the only person who witnessed the intimate ceremony and when asked about the rationale for this, Lear's response was quite practical: she was babysitting Albert's niece so she had no choice but to bring her along. When asked about why the couple did not have a formal wedding ceremony with a bridal gown, family, friends, and other guests, Lear responded that she did not know she was supposed to do all that and just valued marriage so that is what they did. Once this was realized, Lear made a commitment stating that if she and Albert could make it to fifty years of marriage, that they would have a formal vow renewal celebration with their family and friends.

The Detroit Race Riot in 1943 was a result of the rapid migration of blacks from the south into the city and police brutality. With this migration there was a shortage of housing, which was to be addressed by building public housing. The dilemma with this plan was that these public housing developments were scheduled to be built in predominantly white neighborhoods resulting in racial rigidity. Although racial tension was not as openly displayed in the north as it was in the south, this is an example of how racial division, although more silent remained present.

It was in the midst of Jim Crow that Lear and Albert sought to build a new life and traveled to the north landing in the state of New York where Albert had family in 1946. Lear was able to find employment cleaning a hospital but Albert struggled to find sustainable employment, so after one month they traveled to Philadelphia to live with Albert's sister in the pursuit of stable work. Two families managed to live in a one bedroom apartment until Lear and Albert were stable enough to secure their own housing. While Albert landed a job at Yellow Cab Company in the maintenance department, Lear continued to do domestic work for families.

After years of working hard, saving, and sacrificing, Lear and Albert connected with a realtor and made the decision to purchase their first home. In February 1955, they officially became homeowners of a two story row home roughly 1200 square feet between 33rd Diamond and Susquehanna Streets in the Strawberry Mansion section of Philadelphia. Their next door neighbors were also moving in on the same day. All the homes on Diamond Street were occupied by whites except one or two black families. At the time Lear and Albert moved into their home, there were only five or six black families on their street with one being a woman named Blinkie. On the corner of their street was a three story apartment building that later became a garage. Lear describes the entire neighborhood as being occupied by Jewish people.

Albert's young niece thought they had to be the richest people she knew to be able to afford such a beautiful home in an affluent neighborhood with white people, but little did she know that Lear and Albert worked diligently and saved their money to reach their goal. The new home was the perfect location for this young couple because it was right around the corner from their new church. Lear could literally sit on her back porch as the summer wind would breeze through her hair and watch the summer revival service in the church parking lot on a warm August evening while eating a freshly sliced bowl of seeded watermelon.

Lear shared that multiple rooms in the home were covered in wallpaper that was later painted over. The living room and dining rooms had carpet in the center of the rooms, but it was not nailed to the hardwood floor. The kitchen came with a stove, sink, and glass cabinets. The original sink from 1955 was all white, had two silver knobs, an area that could be used for cutting, and storage underneath covered by little doors. Years later when Lear decided to remodel her kitchen, she put that same white sink in the basement where it currently remains. The bathroom had a white clawfoot bathtub. After eleven long years of monthly mortgage payments ranging between from $55 to $60, Lear and Albert finally paid off their home and it was time to celebrate but the celebration did not consist of a party or a trip like one may think. The celebration included remodeling their home, from converting the small kitchen and shed to a larger kitchen, getting a green awning with the initials A.G. on it, and adding a large bay window to allow natural sunlight to enter into the living room.

The two worked long and hard to ensure they were building a lifestyle that they could later enjoy in retirement, but it was not all work with them without some time for play. Albert would graciously drive Lear all around the city from supermarket to supermarket to catch the weekly sales and save money for their household. This frugal shopping on Lear's part allowed the couple to not only build a lifestyle that they could enjoy in retirement but it allowed them to vacation once a year. These vacations included various tropical destinations including Jamaica, Puerto Rico, and the Bahamas to name a few. One day while flying first class from the Bahamas, Lear and Albert had the pleasure of meeting Sidney Portier, a Bahamian American actor, director, and producer who has since received the Presidential Medal of Freedom in 2009. Lear even managed to get Sidney Portier's autograph, which she still has in her possession.

Chapter Three

At the end of 1953, Lear joined the Cornerstone Baptist Church in Philadelphia just one year after the church's origination, following Albert who was already a member. The pastor of the church, Reverend Harold Oliver Davis, was a well known speaker that drew crowds from near and far. Reverend Davis had been described as a gifted preacher, speaker, and talented singer whose love for Christ and passion for teaching God's word drew crowds that worshiped and fellowshipped on Cecil B. Moore Avenue in Philadelphia. Lear became a part of this historic church during the same year that the church was voted into the Pennsylvania Baptist State Convention, whose focus was on following the instructions of Jesus Christ and fellowshipping with one another. Both the Usher Board and Choirs were accepted into the Union and Brotherhood of Philadelphia. This allowed the church to increase its fellowship with the larger community while continuing to learn how to properly practice as a church.

Lear quickly learned that if she did not arrive to Sunday morning service early, there would not be room on the main floor in the sanctuary so she would have to go to the balcony where there would be additional seating. At times, the ushers of the church would place folding chairs in the aisles to allow for more people to sit in the sanctuary and would remove them for offering to ease the flow of traffic as the congregation walked around the aisles. Both Lear and Albert dedicated themselves to serving on various boards, ministries, and auxiliaries within the church and built lifelong friendships. Sunday church services could last the entire day starting with 8am early morning service, followed by 11am service, then an auxiliary's anniversary or a special program at 3pm, and lastly the broadcast, which began at 6pm.

The broadcast consisted of a live church service including the choir singing and the minister of the hour preaching the word of God. This service would be played on the radio for the community to hear every week. Lear remained committed to her church, supporting its multiple endeavors and served in various clubs including the Hospitality Club where the group would fellowship with one another and other churches along with hosting events to raise money for the church including shopping trips, shows, and luncheons. Lear enjoyed this sense of community within her spiritual family and developed friendships that would last for the remainder of her life.

The culture of the church was filled with worship oriented people and those that were eager to serve in whatever capacity they could. There was a sense of order and etiquette within the church. All women were expected to wear skirts that were not form fitting and groups within the church wore a uniform on their designated Sunday on duty. For example, each member of the choir was expected to wear the same attire whether it be a white shirt and black bottom or a standard choir robe on their day to minister through song. The jewelry of a woman was to be modest, such as simple stud earrings or hoop earrings that could not be larger than a quarter. Of course these things were seen as tradition, but it was also to create a sense of order within the church. These traditions were done to encourage modesty and to prevent bringing attention to yourself and away from the ultimate purpose of church service, which included to worship, praise, and learn the word of God. The congregation respected tradition and followed the rules of the church.

Women in the congregation wore formal clothing from three piece suits, either white, black, or nude stockings and hats with all types of decorations from bows, beads, lace and various sizes. Lear describes this attire as her Sunday's best which stems from her childhood. When Lear was a young girl, she would have one nice outfit that was specifically worn for church, therefore as she aged this mentality continued no matter how hot it was outside or in the church. Lear wore a hat of some kind to cover the crown of her head and stockings. The afternoon services would be crowded with people from different churches. After years of dedication and diligence, the congregation moved from Broad and Master Street to their new home at 33rd and Diamond Streets and the Dedicaterial Services were held for ten days ending on the first day of June in 1962. This was a joyous occasion for the entire church congregation and the community as the church was in the heart of North Philadelphia across from Fairmount Park. Since parking was a hot commodity and the church congregation exceeded the parking lot capacity, the congregation was allowed to park across the street at the park and throughout the city block.

After the church found their permanent home, Lear continued her ministry within the church, which included many facets with one being cooking. Lear served as the head of the Culinary Ministry for many years where she was charged with cooking for at least 100 people often times. These meals included pig feet, fried and baked chicken, string beans, collard greens, candied yams, macaroni and cheese, turkey wings, white rice and chicken giblet gravy, and Jiffy cornbread. Lear became well known in the church as an exceptional cook and the church dining room would flood with people on those Sundays it was known that she would be preparing the food. She would prepare these meals for special occasions within the church including the church anniversary, founder's day, and when the Trustee and Trustee Aid Ministries would hold programs on Sunday afternoons. She took great pride in feeding people and seeing the satisfaction on their faces as they ate each bite of their food.

As the head of the culinary ministry, Lear was the point person for purchasing, preparing, and cooking the food for the loved ones of church members who passed away. The church was responsible for paying for all the food and Lear would ask different ministries to donate a cake or pie if possible. As the bereaved family went to the gravesite after the funeral, it was not unusual for some people to stay behind. It was tradition and a sign of respect for everyone to wait until the family arrived back before any food would be served. Once the family arrived and sat down, they would be served by members of the culinary committee first and the rest of the guests would follow. Lear always went above and beyond to ensure that the bereaved family was well taken care of and had plenty of food to take home during their time of bereavement.

The role of the black church was prominent during the Civil Rights Movement, but its prominence did not begin there. During slavery, blacks were only allowed to congregate at church so they relied heavily on their faith in God for the abolishment of slavery and for their freedom. On December 31st, 1862 the first Watch Night Service or better known as "Freedom's Eve" was held where blacks, both free and enslaved, gathered in various churches and homes all over the United States of America, sitting waiting for the news that the Emancipation Proclamation had become law. After everyone received confirmation that they were legally free, there were shouts and prayers of gratitude for finally being free from slavery. It has been over 150 years and the tradition still remains in the black church and each year on December 31st, churches around the nation gather together around 10pm for worship service and to praise God for surviving another year. Roughly ten minutes before the clock strikes midnight, each member of the congregation is invited to get on their knees and pray their way into the new year. The minister then returns to the podium and closes out the prayer where everyone would then rejoice by hugging one another and thanking God for living to see another year.

* * *

The Civil Rights Movement occurred from the mid 1950s to the late 1960s. The Civil Rights Movement was the fight for African American civil rights to include eliminating discriminatory practices to having equal rights like voting without having to go through various extreme measures unlike their counterparts. Lear remembers talking about the Civil Rights Movement among peers but did not let it fully sink in because she had a different experience living in the North. She remembers watching Dr. Martin Luther King, Jr.'s speeches on her black and white television in the living room of her home reporting that everyone cherished him for his nonviolent stance and for shaming those who wanted racial inequality. Lear describes Malcolm X as a person who also stood for civil rights like Dr. King and Rosa Parks as the woman who refused to go to the back of the bus and made it possible for blacks to sit wherever they wanted on public transportation. Lear knew that Dr. King was a prominent person in the Civil Rights Movement and labeled him as her favorite civil rights leader because he stood for "black folks and rights."

Lear described all kinds of mistreatment of blacks by whites while fighting for equal rights such as blacks being stomped at the feet of white people, being hosed down by water hoses, tear gas used to interfere with visibility, being beaten by billy clubs, and even being attacked by dogs during peaceful protests. When Lear and Albert traveled back home to South Carolina to visit their family, they would routinely stop at gas stations to fill the car and stop at places to eat but they could not order food through the front entrance. Instead, Lear would have to walk around to the back of the restaurant and order her and Albert's food at the back window. Once their food was ready she picked it up and the two of them would either have to stand at the back of the restaurant's window to eat it or go to their car to finish their meal. Lear and Albert knew not to go through the front door of the restaurant reporting that two things would have happened: they would have been thrown out of the restaurant or the police would have been called, resulting in a possible arrest. In spite of living up north, Lear and Albert knew, understood, and followed the rules of the south due to fear of persecution.

In 1958, Lear called her younger cousin who lived in South Carolina and asked for her to allow her eight year old daughter to live with her and Albert. Since Lear was the oldest cousin who was established, trusted, and revered there was no hesitation from her cousin to allow the daughter to move to Philadelphia. Lear and Albert traveled by car over nine hours to South Carolina to pick up Lear's second cousin. Although Lear was a second cousin, she was always referred to as Aunt Lear instead of cousin out of respect for her as an elder and because of the age difference since Lear could have been her mother. Although Lear was now residing in the north, the struggle of blacks for freedom was present. It was in 1959 that the Civil Rights Commission noted that both black and whites made the same mistakes on the tests for voting registration but only blacks were denied the opportunity to register to vote.

In August 1959, Dr. Reverend Martin Luther King, Jr. could not attend the church fundraising drive so he sent his dear friend Reverend Ralph Abernathy to stand in his place. This fundraising drive was to help Southern leaders raise funds to get "Negroes" registered and voting. Dr. King also led a multiple city rally in Boston, Chicago, Cleveland, and Philadelphia called the Freedom Now rally in which he addressed a crowd of roughly 10,000 people in Philadelphia in 1965. Although the dates are foggy, Lear and her second cousin remember participating in one of these rallies, marching alongside Reverend Abernathy and other supporters of Dr. King.

Lear became a Trustee Aide after Albert was voted in by members of the church as a Trustee. Both Trustees and Deacons worked alongside the Pastor of the church but in different capacities and were known as the official board of the church. The Deacons were responsible for serving Communion or what is known as The Last Supper and handling spiritual matters while the Trustees were responsible for handling the finances of the church, which included but not limited to collecting, counting, documenting, and depositing all money collected and paying the bills of the church. In the event that the Trustee Board had limited members, the Trustee Aides gladly accepted their role and assisted in these areas. It was tradition to have the Trustees, Trustee Aides, Deacons, and Deaconess' anniversary on the second Sunday of the year during the afternoon service. It was also a tradition to have an installation service during first Sunday afternoon service where all church positions such as the clerk, all presidents, vice presidents, secretaries and so forth for all ministries would be called one by one and would stand around the church in a circle. Once the roll call was complete, a minister would then pray over the leaders being installed in their new roles and the leaders would greet each other by shaking hands as the service concluded.

The congregation of the black church met during the Civil Rights Movement to worship, educate, and teach political advocacy to dismantle the legal systems that enabled blacks to be viewed as inferior while fighting for justice and equality. This fight lasted for decades, but the Civil Rights Movement was different as blacks were more organized in their pursuit of freedom. They went forth making their voices heard while being beaten, incarcerated, or sometimes even facing fatality. These things could not stop them from their fight for equality, in fact the thought of their future grandchildren living in a world where they were judged by the content of their character alone, some may say was enough motivation to keep them going forward to the mark of the high calling. Although protests were peaceful in nature, they were not accepted but instead violence was enforced on them with brutality during protests.

Although black churches demonstrated their voice by peaceful protests, the response to this was violence as evidenced by the Birmingham Church Bombing. The 16th Street Baptist Church was a meeting place for civil rights activities and became a target of violence in Birmingham, Alabama, a city that was already very much segregated. On September 15, 1963 less than an hour before Sunday morning 11am service, a bomb went off caving in the church's interior walls with over twenty people being injured and four fatalities. The four people that died were three 14-year old girls and an 11-year old girl. It took over ten years for the people involved in the bombing to be brought to justice.

In 1985, Cornerstone had their Annual Achievement Awards Luncheon where members of the church were honored for their dedication. In the list of honorees, Lear was presented with the Outstanding Service Award. In the program booklet, there was a black and white picture of her with a short biography that stated, "Lear loves working for the upbuilding of God's Kingdom. She is a Trustee Aide, a member of the Hospitality Auxiliary, Vice President of the Fellowship

Club. She is a Faithful Worker always willing to lend a helping hand at a moment's notice." This was a spot on description of Lear, as she was always willing to do whatever needed to be done in the church, whether it was cleaning and waxing the floors, cooking a meal, or raising money for a special project.

Chapter Four

The term "I have worked all my life" is frequently used by many, but Lear may be the one person who can use that term literally. At the age of thirteen or fourteen years old, Lear began working by taking care of small children between the ages of three to five years old. Lear was able to secure this job through midwives who were looking for someone to take care of a baby for a month or so after their birth. While caring for babies, Lear also worked on the farm making $4.80 per week for her labor and without hesitation she would freely give it to her grandmother to ease her financial burden. Lear would plant cotton then bend over to pick it until her hands were blistered. Cotton was in a ball and would be best picked when it was fluffy so Lear could then pull it out. Cotton was weighed by the pound and when wet it would be heavier, resulting in Lear receiving more money for the wet cotton with dew on it so she would try to pick more of it. Lear would make more than $5 for each pound of cotton and cucumbers.

Once Lear left her grandparents home she continued to do housework and days work making $5 per day. Lear would either find work by looking in the local newspaper or by going to the employment office.

White people would call the employment office looking for a black woman to perform days work, and then the employment office's representative would send someone to the home to work for the day. Lear would work either a 9am-5pm schedule or a 8am-4pm schedule in these homes with no room to slack as she was watched closely by the homeowners. When Lear arrived, she would be greeted by her first name while she was required to greet the adults in the home with Mr. and Mrs. as a sign of respect that was never granted to her. She would also be greeted with what some would call a chore list, naming each thing she would be responsible for completing including but not limited to washing the walls of the home, washing clothes, scrubbing floors, ironing, and making beds. Although Lear was not supposed to be washing walls based on the employment office guidelines, she did what was asked of her to earn the day's pay and for fear of not being asked to return.

There were many days when Lear would climb on a small ladder scrubbing the walls of her employer's home and just as the water was falling down those very walls, her eyes would be filled with tears that would eventually run down her face as she blinked her eyes. The tears she shed were of frustration, anger, and disgust at how she was treated, but she continued to persevere in spite of her circumstances. While working Lear was not allowed to prepare her own lunch in the homes she worked in but instead she would be fed lunch by those who employed her for the day. She was given lunch that consisted of dinner leftovers and scraps that would be fit for dogs, but Lear put her pride aside and completed her work.

During those times, there was no such thing as a mop to clean the floors, so Lear would have to get down on her hands and knees to scrub the floors of these homes. She did this so often that not only would her body be sore but her knees would soon become as black as a cast iron skillet. After working Lear would go home and soak in the bathtub, scrubbing her knees until they would ultimately go back to her regular fair-skinned complexion. Although she did not always feel well and was tired and simply overwhelmed at times, Lear held onto her faith knowing that she could not quit and that brighter days were ahead of her if she only endured those temporary trials and tribulations.

Like in every walk of life there were some employers who were pleasant and others who were spiteful for no precipitating reason. One lady Lear worked for was just dreadful to be around. Lear would dust the white Venetian blinds and move on to cleaning another area of the living room, meanwhile this lady would pull out a white handkerchief and put her finger between the blinds checking for dust to ensure Lear was fully cleaning her home. Lear would witness these undermining actions but would not say a word. No matter how upset Lear became, she always held her composure and let her work speak for her as she was an excellent worker.

The compensation Lear received for a day's work was $5 but she was unable to bring that money home in its entirety because she had to pay 50 cents to the employment office for finding her employment for the day. Lear spent 15 cents a day on transportation which consisted of two tokens for the bus ride. She could ride one bus three or four times by receiving a pass or transfer, which was a small piece of paper that the bus driver would rip off a piece of allowing for another bus ride. After getting off the bus, Lear would sometimes have to walk four or five blocks before arriving at the home of her employer of the day. Lear would bring home $4.35 for an entire day of physical labor and reports being able to survive because things were so cheap back then. A quart of milk was priced at 15 cents and a loaf of bread was 10 cents, so Lear's daily salary would go a long way when it came to purchasing groceries.

Lear started working at Front and Dauphin Streets for a white couple, The Rosenbergs, in 1950. The couple had two children: a son named Dell who was six years old and a daughter named Marlene who was in high school when Lear started. The couple and their family treated Lear well, especially the husband. Mr. Rosenburg would share advice about life with Lear, who absorbed all the information that was offered to her about getting ahead in life. Lear stopped working for this couple after 25 years due to having some medical issues that required her to go to the hospital. Lear swiftly realized that she needed a job with benefits that housework did not provide. To this day, Lear still receives phone calls every once in awhile from the Rosenburg children and the three of them talk for hours reminiscing and providing updates on their lives.

After leaving the Rosenburgs, Lear secured a job in a union but she still worked three days a week doing housework for a woman for extra money. Lear would work at her union job from 9am to 5pm then she would immediately go to her other job doing nighttime cleaning in offices until 2am, with Albert picking her up afterwards. When talking about this Lear asked, "How did I do it? When did I cook?" Lear was not the only one working two jobs, as Albert worked full time for Yellow Cab Company and he worked as a valet driver on the side. One thing about Lear and Albert was that they were both hustlers willing to do whatever they had to do to get ahead in life.

In 1963, Lear began working for Dr. and Mrs. McGill, who had a daughter named Melanie, on City Line Avenue in Bala Cynwyd near Lord and Taylors. Lear was responsible for doing housework and caring for Melanie. When Lear would walk into the house, Melanie would tell her mother to leave, and then she would grab Lear by the hand, guiding Lear to her room and closing the door behind them so Lear could read to her. The McGills often told Lear that she was able to do more with Melanie than they were because Lear was able to discipline her. Lear frequently took Melanie to the playground on the building's site, creating firm boundaries with her regarding what to do and what not to do. When Melanie tested limits, Lear had a switch on top of the refrigerator and would grab it to show Melanie that she was going to get in trouble and receive a spanking. Melanie responded saying, "I'm not gone do it" and Lear had very minimal behavioral issues from Melanie moving forward.

While Lear sat with her close friend, it was revealed that black women would have to line up on 33rd and Diamond Streets, just around the corner from Lear's current home, for whites to pick them as employees to do their housework. If these women were plus sized or had darker skin, they would not be selected. Whites thought that if women were heavier, that they would not work as hard and the colorism of darker versus lighter skinned blacks dates back to slavery when darker skin blacks were known to be field slaves and lighter skin blacks were known to be house slaves, equating to lighter skin being referred to as better than darker skin. This was yet another way for whites to create a division among blacks as if the color of someone's skin meant that they were better. Lear remembers ads in the newspaper that would read similar to this, "Wanted, a position as housekeeper. Must be a respectable, steady, young woman. Must be a first-rate washer and ironer. No dark skin need apply." This was another example of colorism and how black women with lighter skin could either pass for white or be employed as housekeepers more frequently. One may wonder if was due to Lear's very fair skin and jet black hair that she was selected more often than her peers due to perceived notion that she would be a more suitable housekeeper.

Chapter Five

Lear and Albert watched people move in and out of the neighborhood while being respected by all those they encountered. Over the years, they decided to turn the steps of their row home into a porch. Laid on the porch was green carpet with a flower bed shaped like an L in the corner that held various spring flowers and a green awning. Lear took great pride in keeping all the leaves and trash off their property and keeping the street clean as a whole. She would go outside during the street cleaning days, which were typically organized by the block captain at least once a week, to sweep and bag all rubbish. Lear would water her flowers shaped like an L, her hanging plants, and her smaller potted tree in front of her home nightly during the summer heat in hopes of them blossoming beautifully. Albert always drove the finest cars, primarily Cadillacs, and kept them in such pristine condition that people would watch him driving down the street and stare. Albert was able to do this because of him and Lear saving as much money as they could so Albert could pay off the car in three years and save towards a new car, which they purchased every three years.

One night while Lear and Albert slept in the front bedroom of their home they heard someone knocking on their front door. Albert looked out the window and a man who lived in the neighborhood asked if he was the man who had a car in the garage area a few houses down the street. After Albert answered yes, he was told by this neighborhood man that four white men broke into the garage and was trying to steal Albert's car. Albert rushed down the steps and ran out the front door to the garage area only to find that the white men who were attempting to steal his car had already fled. He called the police but no one was ever arrested for the incident. While talking, Lear and Albert began to wonder if the men who attempted to steal his car were some men he worked with at the Yellow Cab Company as they would look at him with an inquisitive stare as Albert rode in his luxurious cars, possibly wondering how a black man could afford such nice cars, prompting the attempted burglary.

Albert with his friendly personality befriended a man who lived four doors down the street. The two men would talk frequently and discuss cars as Albert was always fond of cars, keeping them up to date with maintenance and clean on both the inside and outside. Albert's cars would shine as if they were coming fresh from the dealership and the inside remained free from debris and trash of any sort. The man who Albert befriended was married to a woman named Mary who Lear described as not as friendly as her husband. Lear remembers Mary as being a woman almost 40 years her junior who was from New York City. Mary left her family at eighteen years old and moved to Philadelphia, eventually buying a house next door to her great aunt Blinkie who was one of the few blacks who lived on the street years prior. Mary moved to Philadelphia to make a life for herself, her husband, and later her two daughters. Mary seemingly stayed to herself and kept her two daughters dressed in beautiful clothing like lace dresses, white stockings, and patent leather dress shoes with their hair neatly braided with bows and barrettes. Lear always admired how attentive Mary was to her daughters and how she took pride in their appearance.

Mary always had a genuine love for older adults as she was concerned for their safety as a child when the police were going on strike and the only thing Mary was concerned about was who would be there to protect the senior citizens of New York City. Later, as an adult, Mary became a home health aide for a major home care agency that originated in Philadelphia so she respected Lear and Albert as they were her elders. Since Mary's family primarily lived in New York aside from a great aunt and great uncle who lived next door to her, Lear took a motherly watch over Mary and the two became very close as time progressed. Mary also later joined Cornerstone Baptist Church with her daughters.

As Mary would become homesick and miss her biological family, she would call her mother asking about her coming to visit. Mary's mother would insist she go down the street and spend some time with Lear as Lear became a trusted part of Mary's family with her motherly influence. There were countless times where Mary would be faced with a tough decision regarding her life or something pertaining to her children and would seek guidance from Lear.

Mary and Lear would spend time bonding by going on shopping trips to the local thrift store on the days where there was a senior discount so Mary could save extra money and stock up on pajamas, essentials for her young daughters, and the finest dishes in brand new or mint condition. Lear's church groups would host trips to Englishtown Auction Sales, which was often referred to as just Englishtown, in Elizabeth, New Jersey. Englishtown was a flea market approximately an hour and thirty minutes from the church. Groups within the church would meet to discuss fundraisers and Englishtown was always at the top of the list. The group would secure a coach bus that would seat a little over fifty people and agree on a date for the trip. Each member of the group would be responsible for selling a certain amount of tickets, but Lear being the socialite that she was always sold more than the allotted amount. Once tickets were sold it was time to prepare for the shopping adventures. The shopping trip would typically consist of primarily women, often members of the church looking to shop for anything, everything, or nothing in particular.

On the day of the trip all the people would gather on the bus, pray for safe travels, sometimes collect a donation for the bus driver, and serve refreshments consisting of juice, danishes, and donuts. Once the group arrived at Englishtown, the group leader would announce to the entire bus what time everyone had to arrive back and whether or not the bus driver would be available for people to bring their purchased items throughout the day, then the races were off. Lear and Mary would grab their purses and head off to shop at the flea market where they saw antiques, plants, collectibles, clothing, jewelry, speciality food, home decor from wall art to rugs, and so much more. After hours of walking Lear and Mary would have worked up an appetite and stop for a bite to eat then shop some more. Even when they came back from shopping nearly empty handed, it was still a joyous bonding experience when the two of them spent time together.

It was a tradition in the Green household for a specific meal to be served on Fridays. This meal was a tradition Lear maintained from South Carolina during childhood that she carried throughout her adulthood. During the week, Lear's family would eat meat but on Fridays the family would eat seafood. This meal consisted of hand breaded fried fish, fried shrimp, hush puppies, homemade red rice, either cabbage or collard greens, cornbread, and homemade sweet tea. As the two of them would eat this delicious meal, Albert would joke stating that they can have fish and grits in the morning for breakfast if Mary did not come down and eat up all their food. It seemed like shortly after that, Mary would ring the bell and both Lear and Albert would laugh as they shared the joke with Mary who laughed as she washed her hands in the kitchen sink and made herself a hearty plate. As the years would pass, Lear and Mary got closer and closer. Mary saw Lear as a mother figure as she offered her motherly love, support, guidance and encouragement.

In 1989, Mary became pregnant with her third child who she hoped would be the son she had always wanted, and this pregnancy like the other two resulted in her being sick and spending weeks off and on in the hospital. Lear stepped in along with Mary's family and took care of her daughters until she finally returned home. After weeks of sickness Mary gave birth to a beautiful baby girl who she named Symoné. Lear naturally was drawn to this new baby considering her relationship with Mary. Although Symoné was born 20 days early, she was healthy and did not need to spend any extra time in the hospital.

Mary cherished her children and took her responsibility of parenting seriously including the importance of raising her children in the church. One tradition of the church is to have a baby dedication shortly after the birth of a child. A baby dedication is a ceremony typically performed by the Pastor, minister, or deacon of the church where the baby's parents are committing themselves to raising the child in a Godly way until the child is able to make the decision to follow God for themselves. This tradition stems from the story of Hannah in the Holy Bible where Hannah did not bear children and desperately prayed to God pleading her case and requesting to have a son that she would give completely to God for a life of holy discipline. After years of Hannah's heart yearning for a child, she became pregnant and gave birth to a son. After she received what she so desperately longed for, Hannah kept her word to God and dedicated her son back to God.

During a baby dedication the parents are giving their child back to God as it is believed by Christians that children are given as a gift from God that is to be given back to Him for discipleship. The baby dedication for Symoné took place when she was six months old and was held in front of the church at the altar. Symoné was dressed in an all white dress covered in lace and a white bonnet to represent innocence and purity. The associate minister at the time came to the altar and called for Symoné's parents to come forward. The minister asked for the family to come forward as well. "It takes a village to raise a child" is an African proverb that holds true in the church. The church is considered to be a family for a child as children need both a biological family to handle the earthly needs and a spiritual family to raise a child with the appropriate spiritual upbringing, guidance, and influence. It was at that time that Lear silently walked to the altar before the church congregation standing with Mary, Symoné's father, and the rest of the family for the baby dedication ceremony.

After the ceremony was over Mary, her family, and friends went back to her home for an early dinner. As Mary was frying chicken, her friends were in the living room but it was fairly quiet resulting in Mary wondering if they were asking each other who was Symoné's Godmother. It was at that moment that Mary received a call from Lear where she confirmed that her and "Uncle Albert" as she affectionately called him were going to be Symoné's godparents. Mary told Lear that she had a lot of family and that she did not have to worry about it but Lear insisted so Mary ended the conversation and announced to all her guests that Mr. & Mrs. Green were going to be Symoné's godparents and just like that the tension in the living room ceased. However Lear remembers Mary asking her and Albert to be Symoné's godparents which is why Lear stood with the family during the dedication ceremony and officially accepted the request later that day via phone. Either way, Lear had no idea what she signed up for, but it was a life changing decision for both her and Symoné.

Chapter Six

Lear played an integral part of Symoné's life and by living down the street she became closer to Lear than her biological grandparents. When Mary was ready to return to work, she consulted with Lear about who would care for Symoné. Lear suggested a woman who lived across the street who was nearly 70 years old, had watched her family's children while they worked, and recently began raising her two great granddaughters. Lear advised Mary to ask this woman and said between her and the woman that Symoné would be well taken care of. The woman graciously accepted and Mary was able to return to work. Symoné was four years old when she was tested by the public school district for kindergarten and passed the test. On the first day of school, Mary dressed Symoné in an all white button down shirt, a black and white plaid skirt, a red checkered vest, white stockings, black shoes with ponytails and barrettes to match her outfit while Lear stood alongside smiling with pride and excitement. The two cheered Symoné on for beginning a new chapter in her life while they took pictures with a black Polaroid camera that instantly printed out the picture. This picture remains on Lear's refrigerator as a reminder of that special day.

Once Symoné was old enough to walk around the corner from school independently, she would pass by her house and come straight to see her Godparents. Often times Lear would be in the kitchen preparing a delicious dinner so Symoné would pull out her school books and complete her homework while patiently waiting for dinner to be served. During those times Symoné would inquire about how to prepare foods, why certain seasonings were used and would become Lear's personal taste tester sampling each item or better yet just eating because Lear's food did not require any adjustments for flavor. Symoné quickly learned that measurements were not often used by Lear for cooking, but only for baking, and that seasonings were sprinkled into the food and then tasted to see if more was needed to improve the taste. This was the way Lear was raised to prepare food by her grandmother and it held true throughout the years.

During Symoné's formative years she would wait until Friday night and pack an overnight bag to go spend the night with Lear and Albert. As Symoné did this, one of her sisters would laugh and tease her about how hype she was to only go down the street to be with her Godmother. It became a routine for her to ask her parents for permission to spend the night, but she quickly realized that her father was more lenient so she would ask him instead of her mother who always ensured all chores in the house were done before agreeing to allow Symoné to spend the night. Of course, Symoné's mother and father would talk and the next time Symoné would ask her father to spend the night she was shocked when he told her to go ask her mother. Being sneaky, Symoné would write a note to her mother stating "Can I spend the night at Godmother's?" with YES being in large big bold writing and the word no being so small it could not even be detected on the paper. Symoné would wait until her mother was on the phone talking to her family in New York or watching a movie and hand the note to her. When Mary would read the letter she would laugh at Symoné's creative way to get what she wanted and at the perfect timing when Mary was distracted.

Most times, the answer was yes so Symoné would tell her father that Mary allowed her to go and he would walk her to the door as she eagerly ran down the street where her Godmother would greet her at the door with a smile and wave goodbye to Symoné's father. Lear enjoyed Symoné's company and the two would spend most of their time together in the kitchen watching television, cooking, and cleaning up the aftermath. Symoné knew the routine, after getting the approval she would walk into her Godparents house, snack a little with her Godmother then go upstairs to get ready for bed. After washing up she would open the second drawer of the cherry wood dresser covered with a glass finish to protect the wood to get her clean underclothes and designated nightgown for bed before jumping in the bed. Symoné would sleep in the back bedroom with Lear and her french toy poodle Fluffy in a queen sized bed.

One day Lear stayed downstairs late cleaning up the kitchen after dinner so instead of Symoné going upstairs to bed alone she fell asleep on the washer and dryer in the corner of the kitchen trying to stay up for her Godmother. Lear picked Symoné up and carried her all the way to the bedroom, changed her into a nightgown and carefully put her into bed not to wake her. Another night Lear was up late doing laundry and as she approached the steps to go to the second floor of her home she looked at her poodle and asked, "Fluffy, do you want to walk upstairs or do you want Mommy to carry you?" To Symoné's surprise Fluffy stood on her hind legs as if she was begging for Lear to carry her upstairs so Lear did just that while Symoné carried the freshly washed and folded white clothes up the stairs. Fluffy was more of Lear's child than her dog as Lear would tell Fluffy to come to the phone and talk to her friend who watched Fluffy while Lear and Albert were away on vacation. Fluffy would slowly come from the foot of the bed and sit still as Lear held the phone to her ear as the friend on the phone talked. Sometimes at night Symoné would tussle with Fluffy to see who would be the one to sleep the closest to Lear who hysterically laughed at the gesture.

After school Lear and Symoné would watch Lear's soap operas or as she called them her "stories," especially Guiding Light, which came on weekdays at 3pm. Symoné would watch the second half considering she would get out of school at 3:04pm. Other shows the two of them watched were Matlock, Murder She Wrote, Walker Texas Ranger, and Touched by an Angel. Matlock featured a man who paid great detail to investigating every aspect of evidence while solving cases as a criminal defense lawyer. Murder She Wrote focused on an amateur detective and is classified as a crime drama series. Walker Texas Ranger was an action crime television series. It always amused Symoné that the main character, Walker, would fight one or more villains with punches and spinning kicks but his cowboy hat would never come off his head. Touched by an

Angel featured three angels who traveled to Earth to inspire people to turn to God while learning life's lessons themselves. Touched by an Angel always seemed to be one of Lear's favorites since it was a faith based show.

There were times when Lear would take Symoné with her to run errands using public transportation primarily during the summer months. Since Lear was over 65, she was classified as a senior citizen and was able to ride public transportation for free as long as she showed the driver her senior citizen pass. Children on the other hand needed to pay if they were taller than a specific height that was displayed at the front of the bus. Lear being savvy had Symoné stoop down bending her knees to appear shorter than she was to prevent paying for her as she entered the bus at the front entrance.

Lear and Albert went out to eat often on Sundays and would take Symoné with them, especially to The Pub in New Jersey because children ate for free that day. This restaurant can seat at least 300 people and Symoné became a regular with Lear, Albert, and their friends. Another favorite restaurant of Lear's was Old Country Buffet where she would typically load her plate with salad and all the fixings followed by a bowl of soup. After eating all that Lear would seldom have enough room for more than one small plate of food. Old Country Buffet offered a discounted rate for children which was based on the age of the child. Employees at the front of the buffet who were responsible for collecting the money would ask the children how old they were instead of the adults in hopes of receiving a more honest answer, but Symoné quickly learned this and would ask Lear before getting to the register, "Godmother, how old am I today?" Lear would glance at the price guidelines for children and tell Symoné her age for the day. Although Symoné had a large appetite she was able to pass for younger for years due to being thin and small in stature. After eating a belly full as Lear called it, Symoné would come home and tell her mother all about her dinner with her Godparents, including how she asked Lear her age and went along with whatever Lear told her for that instance alone. When Mary heard this all she could do was laugh and then call and tease Lear for always finding a way to save a dollar.

* * *

Lear wanted to work until 65 for full social security benefits but decided to retire at age 63 because Albert nagged her to stop working since he had already retired. To keep busy after her formal retirement, Lear was hired to work only on Wednesdays by an older woman who wanted someone to look after the home in which her middle aged son lived in. Lear would go into the home weekly and tidy up the living space, leaving her plenty of time to spend with Albert and Symoné. When Symoné was not in school she would ride along with Albert to pick Lear up from work often times with Fluffy. This became somewhat of a routine, but Lear slowly began to notice changes as things would soon take a turn.

Looking back, Lear recalls how things would happen but she did not pay it much attention as Albert would drop her off at work in the morning and Lear would get off at 1pm expecting Albert to be outside waiting for her. Albert would tell Lear as he picked her up that he would have to drive all the way back home and start out again to find his way to her job. There were also times when Lear would return home after waiting so long for Albert only to find that he was not home. As Lear noticed these patterns she took Albert to his scheduled primary care physician appointment where Albert was diagnosed with Alzheimer's disease, which is a form of dementia. Dementia is a broad term that refers to the decline in memory and functioning level that has been described in three primary types: Lewy body, vascular, and the most common one being Alzheimer's disease. Alzheimer's disease is a progressive condition that accounts for nearly 80% of dementia cases where individuals have plaques in their brain that cause nerve damage. This nerve damage impacts one's ability to function in their everyday life and can result in wandering, forgetting to turn the stove off, forgetting to eat, and incongruent body temperature.

Without continuous support, individuals who have been diagnosed with dementia can be at risk in the community. Lear did not share the formal diagnosis with Albert at the time his physician made the determination. Albert's physician also stated that he was no longer able to continue driving due to safety concerns including getting lost and being susceptible to people taking advantage of him due to his cognitive impairment. Learning about Albert's condition was life altering for Lear, but she followed the doctor's orders and with the help of Mary, she removed his car keys from his key ring to prevent Albert from potentially being taken advantage of or any further incidents of wandering. Lear decided to leave Albert with his key ring that included his house keys to still allow him to have the independence of having his keys on his personal body. Surprisingly Albert was not as upset about having his car keys taken off his key ring, but Lear was considering she no longer had the luxury of Albert driving her around the city to run errands but deep down inside she knew this decision was the best decision to ensure Albert's safety.

Albert began to change right before Lear's eyes. He no longer wanted to follow his daily routine of getting up early in the morning, getting dressed, eating breakfast, and going out to run errands. Albert became content with laying in the bed all day if Lear would not insist on him getting up. Lear became Albert's caregiver and at that point she took her wedding vows "for better or worse" and "in sickness and in health" seriously and dedicated herself to caring for Albert no matter what it took. For example, Lear would leave the home around 8am to go to the grocery store, the dry cleaners, and run other errands then she would arrive back home by 11am. Once she entered the home, Albert would hear the chimes on the vestibule door and greet Lear from his bedroom. She would then call upstairs sometimes several times for Albert to get washed up and come downstairs for breakfast. Lear would always make a hearty breakfast such as bacon, grits, stewed tomatoes, and eggs for Albert. Other times she would make fried porgy fish, grits, homemade biscuits with orange marmalade jelly, and coffee. Although Albert's memory was impacted, it was primarily his short term memory that was affected. He was always able to remember Lear, Symoné, Mary, and her two other daughters but could not remember if or what he had for breakfast. There were often times when Symoné would ask Albert what he had for breakfast during the middle of the day and his response would be nothing, so Symoné would gently remind him what he ate and he was always apologetic and trusting of what she told him. This was a little test Symoné would perform to see if Albert's memory was improving, but unfortunately for nearly ten years Albert's memory remained the same. Unlike some stories of people with Alzheimer's disease, Albert remained pleasant throughout his journey with dementia. Other people who have loved ones who have been diagnosed with dementia have difficulty with their loved ones leaving the home and wandering in the streets thinking they are going to work, to see family members, or run errands. On the other hand, Albert was content with staying in the house with no one to bother him. Lear placed chimes on the vestibule door as an added precaution. If Albert attempted to leave the home, Lear would be able to hear these chimes and catch him before he could leave.

One day, Symoné's oldest sister and her husband came to visit Lear and Albert. While Symoné's sister went into the kitchen her husband sat in the living room asking Albert if he knew who he was and Albert answered no. As time passed Albert called Symoné's brother in law by his name stating to tell his wife that he was hungry. As Symoné's brother in law turned in shock he stated, "Pop Pop, I thought you didn't know who I was." Albert laughed and said, "Of course I know you." This was just a small example of how Albert maintained his jovial personality no matter what his limitations were. Albert was often specific in what he wanted for dinner stating, "Lear, make me a steak" and Lear graciously would do so only for Albert to take a few mouthfuls of food then say he was full. Since Lear knew Albert's limitations, she would firmly encourage Albert to keep eating because he only had one meal that day. Lear also knew that Albert's mind may be telling him he is full but he could be malnourished due to the incongruent connection between his mind and body. Lear would eat her food and literally feed Albert until at least 75% of his food was finished followed by an option of dessert whether it was homemade pie or cake, a danish, coffee, and/or tea.

Symoné recalls her nieces who were toddlers asking to go to the bathroom upstairs, then running back down crying saying they were scared. After much discussion, they realized that Albert was making some of the ugliest faces at the children with his eyes enlarged, his tongue sticking out, and his hands on his head near his temple to scare them. When Albert was caught by Symoné and Lear, he laughed, saying he was just playing with the kids then stopped after Lear insisted for him to do so.

Although Albert's short term memory remained stagnant, his long term memory was quite impressive as he would remember people who he met over twenty years ago and could describe them down to the sound of their voice or prominent features. To keep Albert engaged and his mind active, Lear encouraged him to watch television, especially the news, but little did she know the television ended up watching him. Symoné saw how Lear tried to engage Albert so she decided to do things on her own to promote interactions and stimulate his mind. In the basement of their home was an old checkers board that was handmade by an older gentleman who lived across the street. Symoné would often beg Albert to play checkers with her which he agreed to do since he could not say no to his goddaughter asking, "What am I going to do with you" only to have Symoné respond saying, "You could throw me out the window but that wouldn't be nice." Lear would watch the two of them playing checkers and smile with pride as Symoné looked up to Albert and saw him as a father figure.

Since his diagnosis of dementia, Albert was not interested in shaving his beard or going to the barbershop for a routine haircut so Lear would ask Symoné, who was about nine or ten years old at the time, to walk Albert to Bob's Barber Shop about four blocks away. Early Saturday morning, Lear would make sure Albert took a shower and ate breakfast then she would give Symoné four quarters out of her silver jar in the dining room to grab snacks on her way to Bob's. The first few times Symoné walked Albert to the barbershop he asked to take a break sitting on the steps of the brownstone apartment building due to being tired. This break could be twenty minutes followed by difficulty getting Albert to stand up. Symoné swiftly learned how to be efficient so she would walk Albert to the barbershop without allowing for any breaks, observe the number of people in front of him to ensure he would not miss his spot in line, and then go to the corner store for snacks.

When she returned, she would sit in the barbershop with men and boys of all ages and watch either Sanford and Son or Good Times while savoring her salty and sweet treats. Once it was Albert's turn, the barber would lean the chair back, lather up his face with shaving cream, and gently slide the straight edge razor across his face and neck removing all hair and trimming his mustache. At the end of the shave, the barber would place a warm hand towel across his face and just like that Albert looked like a brand new man. Symoné would offer Albert compliments and the two would walk hand and hand back home to show Lear and get her stamp of approval. During those rare times when Symoné was unable to walk Albert to the barbershop, Lear would call the barber who they had developed a friendship with over the years and explain the situation. The barber would graciously offer to come to their home and shave Albert which Lear appreciated.

In the summer months, Symoné would be home with her older sisters who were seven and ten and a half years older than her, who were often out on their own. Symoné would wake up, make her bed, and complete the assigned tasks her mother left for her, which would include dusting the coffee tables, cleaning her room, or folding clothes that Mary may have started laundering before she left for work in the morning. Once all tasks were completed, she would turn off all the lights and lock both locks on the front door then walk down the street to spend some quality time with her godparents. Since Symoné could not cook at home without her mother's supervision due to fear of a fire or other complications, she would ask her Godmother if she could make breakfast, which Lear gladly allowed.

Symoné would wash her hands in the kitchen sink, go into the refrigerator, open a tray and pulled out some Oscar Mayer bacon. She would place two to three strips of bacon on the bacon tray in the microwave, set it to five minutes and press start. Once the bacon was started, Symoné would pour pancake mix into her favorite glass mixing bowl that was white with a handle and had flowers all around it. Symoné would not measure the pancake mix so sometimes she ended up with three pancakes and other times she had nearly six. Lear always allowed Symoné to be independent while cooking or at least gave that illusion as Lear would insert reminders such as add a little butter and once the holes are on the pancake mix it's time to flip them. Once the food was all done, Symoné would sit down at the six person table with her pancakes, bacon, and old fashioned syrup that was kept at the bottom of the turntable in the corner of the kitchen and pour it over the pancakes and bacon. This particular syrup was from Lear's hometown so it was rich and tasty. Lear would sit at the table smiling at Symoné and she would do a little dance rocking back and forth while eating her food.

On June 26, 2001, Symoné asked her parents to spend the night with her Lear and Albert and they obliged her. The following morning Symoné woke up, got dressed, and looked outside the front door where she saw her sister and infant niece coming down the street. She then saw her mother and paternal aunt drive down the street. This was unusual for Mary who typically worked until the late afternoon. Symoné shortly learned that her father had a massive heart attack leading to his demise. It was at that point she thought her life was beginning to shatter.

As the days, weeks, and months passed her relationship with Lear and Albert remained consistent. Lear was always there to comfort Symoné when she tried to make sense out of her father's death and spoil her when she wanted to be a brat. Albert continued to shower Symoné with his love and support saying time and time again that, "No man will make a fool of Symoné." This was said because not only did Symoné's father and godfather teach her how a man was supposed to treat his woman, but her mother and Godmother would not accept anything less than the best, so Symoné learned by observation. Symoné watched the relationship of Albert and Lear and it was evident that the two of them had a special connection that was only found once in a lifetime.

Symoné continued to ask her mother to spend the night with her godparents but that would leave Mary alone for the most part, so in the middle of the night Mary would call the Green residence and say open the door because she was coming down too. Lear would turn the hallway light on and walk down the fifteen steps to unlock and open her doors and let Mary in calling her a "chicken butt" because she did not want to stay in her home alone. The three of them would laugh about this, grab a late night snack, and head to bed.

Chapter Seven

After years of living on Natrona Street, raising her three children, and watching the neighborhood deteriorate with drug infiltration, crime, and residents with a questionable moral compass, Mary made a difficult decision and began her new housing search. In February 2004, Mary and Symoné moved to a better neighborhood after Mary purchased a three bedroom, 1.5 bathroom home in the Northwest section of Philadelphia in an area known as East Mount Airy. Mary owned her home on Natrona Street, so she allowed her middle daughter to live in that home with her two children. Symoné was hesitant to move considering she would be leaving many things behind: the only home she knew, her godparents, her sister and two nieces, the convenience of her church being around the corner, and the one bus commute to her high school, but as a child the decision was made for her and the move was beyond her control.

Mary would catch two out of three buses with Symoné to make sure she was safe going to school but since Mary understood Symoné's desire to remain in her familiar setting she allowed Symoné to stay majority of the time with her Godparents. By this time, Lear moved to the middle bedroom on a twin bed across from Albert resulting in Symoné having a queen sized bed and the entire back bedroom to herself. Since Symoné basically lived with Lear and Albert, she would set an alarm on her cell phone every day for school, followed by Mary calling her every morning to ensure she was awake and dressed for school as Mary valued many things including education and punctuality. Each morning after Symoné showered and watched the weather on 6 Action News she kissed Lear on her cheek as Lear was partially sleep saying goodbye and letting her know that she was leaving for school. Lear would either tell Symoné to take a few dollars for lunch money that she either laid out the night before or Symoné would be told to take from a special silver dish that held quarters in the dining room. Mary would check in with Symoné to make sure she made it to school safely and after school to make sure she made it home safe. During their evening calls, Mary ensured her homework was completed and pry about every detail of her school day along with making sure she was in bed at a reasonable time. Mary would even come to the Green residence on Sundays before church as she continued her membership at Cornerstone and would spend the night during the week.

In early August 2005, Albert had gastrointestinal issues for a few days leading to Lear taking him to the emergency room where the attending physician recommended surgery. Before Mary could arrive at the hospital to evaluate and offer her insight into the situation, Lear had already decided for Albert to have the surgery. The surgery landed Albert in the Intensive Care Unit where he was hooked up to all kinds of machines and was unable to talk due to tubes down his throat. At Albert's bedside was Lear, Mary, and Symoné who could not believe how quickly things had turned. Lear listened attentively to the doctor's reports and Mary asked questions to clarify what happened during surgery and what the family should expect, but Symoné just stood in disbelief. Since Albert had dementia for years, Symoné knew his cognitive limitations but to see her godfather in a hospital bed unable to speak or move crushed her.

When Lear's friend heard about Albert's condition she went to the hospital and while getting out of the car at the front of the hospital, she lost her balance and fell. While trying to brace herself for the fall she broke both her wrists and was later admitted to the same hospital. Lear and Symoné went to the hospital daily to see Albert praying that he would recover and return home. Symoné remained optimistic that Albert would be home soon and in the interim, Lear decided to have a new olive green carpet put in the middle room where Albert slept as a welcome home gift.

On Wednesday August 24th, Lear, Mary, and Symoné waited in the waiting room while Albert was being bathed by the hospital team who later came to tell Lear that Albert's heart had stopped and he had to be revived. The hospital asked Lear to make a decision of what to do in the event this happened again. It was at that point the reality began to sink in and Lear decided to go to God in prayer before making her decision. When the family was able to go back in the room to see Albert, Symoné made it her business to speak to her Pop Pop as she did not have the chance to say goodbye to her father but she needed to speak her peace to her godfather while she had the chance.

Symoné cautiously walked into Albert's room with her eyes filled with tears, sat on a small portion at the foot of Albert's bed, and held his swollen right hand. She cried and poured out her heart to her godfather, thanking him for everything he had done for her, that she appreciated him and loved him more than she could ever express. Since Albert was unable to talk, she asked him to squeeze her hand if he heard her and just a few seconds later he did so. This created a sense of ease and comfort, knowing that she was able to thank a man who gave her so much over her fifteen years of life. Lear was able to speak to Albert and consulted Mary about the decision she had to make, but she knew that Albert had lived a long life and that he was suffering in his present state so she agreed that she would not interfere with God's will, meaning that if Albert's heart stopped again then God made the decision to end his life and to call him home to Heaven.

The next day, Symoné was coming out of the front bedroom at Lear and Albert's home when Lear was walking into the middle bedroom as she told Symoné "When Uncle Albert dies, you gone have to help me get the house ready for the family." Symoné, in disbelief, told her Godmother that Pop Pop was not going to die. As Symoné looked into Lear's eyes she saw nothing but pain as Lear stated that Uncle Albert was going to die and that she would need Symoné's help to tidy up the house in preparation to receive the family when Albert passed. Although Symoné was always willing to help her godmother in any way, she could not understand how her Godmother could even speak words of Albert's death but little did she know Lear was mature in her walk with Christ. She understood the need to accept God's will no matter if it did not align with her own.

On Friday, August 26th, Symoné went to the last day of the annual youth revival at Cornerstone Baptist Church where the sermon gave her an epiphany that she was being selfish by not letting Albert go, so she prayed for peace, acceptance, and strength to help her Godmother get through such a difficult time with losing her husband of almost sixty-two years. On Saturday, August 27th, Lear as usual woke up early and caught multiple buses alone to see Albert in the hospital. Symoné went to church for choir rehearsal and was planning to visit her godfather afterwards. Symoné received a call from her mother while she was on her way to the hospital telling her to come to the hospital quick as Pop Pop's heart rate was going down and he did not have much time left. Symoné, filled with anxiety, moved as quickly as she could to go to the hospital but there were bus detours resulting in the bus seemingly stopping at every corner and delaying her getting to the hospital.

When Symoné arrived at the hospital she rushed to the Intensive Care Unit, picked up the phone, and gave her Godfather's name to the nurse who answered and was buzzed in. Symoné was relieved, thinking she made it to the hospital in time but as she walked in the room she saw all the machines removed but did not think anything of it. As Symoné continued to walk into the room she saw her mother had her back to the door as she was looking out the window at the Philadelphia skyline. When Mary heard Symoné walk in she turned around and Symoné noticed that her eyes were bloodshot red so instantly she knew her Godfather had passed away. Symoné rushed to her godfather's bedside and began to cry loudly. Her mother held her as she was grief stricken.

When Symoné calmed down, Mary asked where Lear was so Symoné let her know that Godmother must have been on another floor of the hospital visiting her girlfriend with the broken wrists. Shortly thereafter, Lear walked through the door and began crying as she knew Albert had passed just one day before their 62nd anniversary and his 90th birthday. After the initial shock of Albert's death, Lear, Mary, and Symoné caught a cab to Lear's home. Mary helped Lear every step of the way as funeral arrangements were being made and it was included in Albert's obituary that Mary was his God-Given daughter.

Chapter Eight

Technology has evolved over the last century including multiple inventions registered and patented since the 1920s. Garrett Augustus Morgan, a man of African descent was born to slaves and invented the electric automatic traffic signal after witnessing two cars crashing into one another. The electronic automatic traffic signal was designed to ease the flow of traffic and allowed a break in changing lights after automobiles stopped at red lights and before pedestrians walked across the street as a built in protection when automobiles ran lights. Also during this year, John Harwood, an English, man registered his invention which was the first self-winding watch. This watch used the motion from the person wearing the watch to maintain its energy and keep time. James Cummings and J. Earl McLeod invented the first bulldozer, which was a machine with a blade on the front that was used to push massive amounts of material typically during construction. While we now have the ability to take photographs that print instantly, this would have not been possible without Samuel Shalfrock who invented the earliest instant camera which included a camera and a portable darkroom in one compartment.

As a child, Lear did not know anything about different forms of entertainment such as the radio or television as the television was not invented until 1925. Although the phone was invented in the mid-1800s and the radio was invented in the late-1800s, Lear's family had no first hand experience with these methods of communication due to living in poverty. In fact, there was little to no communication with others outside of the home and limited visitation with family members who did not live nearby. The only form of entertainment known to Lear as a child was talking to the people in her home.

To travel, Lear and her grandparents did not have a car; they used a horse and buggy or a cart to haul wood or other supplies for their farm. The family did not even have a clock in the home nor did they know what a clock was during that time. Lear's grandparents learned to tell the time by simply looking up at the sun then down at their shadow. Lear laughed as she described this stating it sounds funny but "them old folks knew how to tell time," so much that she was never late for school. Lear did not see her first stove until her aunt passed away, resulting in that stove being brought into the family home. She did not have an ice box or a refrigerator to store meat, vegetables, or other food. Instead the family would make just enough food for that meal and would eat it all to eliminate having leftovers as it would quickly spoil.

Early in the 1900s, private homes began having running water in the home but considering the poverty Lear was raised in, she didn't experience this. Since there was no running water in the home, Lear would carry a small bucket to get water from the nearby well. This water was used by Lear to drink, wash her body, and/or to wash dishes. There were different sizes of tubs that were used for different purposes such as bathing and washing clothes with the larger tub being used by Lear to wash her body. When she wanted to take a warm bath she would carry the large tub outside and sit it in the sun to warm the water naturally.

Lear has watched technology from its inception from cars to computers and everything in between. Ford Motor Company was founded by Henry Ford on June 16, 1903. The Model T was sold by Ford Motor Company from 1908 to 1927 and was the first car some people were able to purchase due to its affordability and steel structure which eased travel on paved roads. Not only was the Model T affordable, but it was long lasting. The Model T had five styles including a five-seat touring car that had an open build with mini doors and a roof that covered the passengers similar to a convertible that comes up and down. The windshield was a glass or plastic structure that sat in front of the steering wheel but had nothing on the sides to hold it in place. Instead the front windshield was held in place at the top of the bumper. The earlier models had non-demountable wheels and as time progressed the wheels became demountable. This car was produced exclusively in black before 1925, had a 4 cylinder engine that allowed the car to go 40-45 miles per hour costing $850. Vehicles have since transformed with Ford still having one of the top ratings in 2019. It is not required that vehicles are purchased at a dealership anymore as they can be purchased via phone or even using the computer with customization from the color, seating, engine size, type of rims for tires, or even the accessories for the trunk such as carpet or a cargo net. Vehicles also range in price with more luxury vehicles costing around $100,000. Lear has watched the entire evolution of the automobile over the course of her life.

When going to the grocery store as a young adult, there was an electronic cash register that was color coded with specific colors to indicate clerk keys, departments including taxes, coins, paper money, and so forth. The cash register was responsible for transactions involving addition only and was not designed for refunds or payouts. At the top of the register, the cash amount due was largely displayed for Lear to see as she gave the cashier cash. There was a larger button on the side that when hit would open the register to allow the cashier to distribute change as needed. There are now three different types of cash registers including the electric cash register models, the battery-operated cash register, and portable cash registers. Some of these models ease the process of tracking transactions. With these registers and the evolution of technology, all items in the grocery stores now have a barcode. As Lear remembers going to the market, she notices that the barcode on items are used to scan at the register to give cashiers the price of the item. In larger stores, there is a reduction in cashiers and an increase in self-checkout lines where Lear could scan each of her items and pay using a machine.

This stage of technology is a bit much for Lear, so she sticks to the old fashioned way of doing things and visits the cashier. Now Lear has the luxury of not having to carry cash to pay for her daily purchases partly because of technology and for safety reasons. It took her some time to get used to the idea of paying for items using an electronic payment instead of cash. When Symoné started mentioning the safety concerns related to a senior citizen having cash in public, Lear began to consider the need for using a card. Symoné went with Lear to her local grocery stores and gently taught her how to use her cards to pay for items. Once she showed Lear how to either swipe or insert her cards with a security chip and which buttons to push on the card reader to accept the payment, Lear became a professional doing so independently.

Although change is inevitable, changes in technology have happened so rapidly that it has been challenging for Lear to keep up. Years ago when Lear wanted to call a friend, she could pick up the phone that was attached to the wall where she would dial seven numbers to contact her local friends and family. If Lear wanted to place a long distance phone call, she would have to dial a one in front of the number after hearing the dial tone. If there were questions about a phone number, Lear could simply pick up the phone and dial zero to speak to an operator who would answer her questions and connect her to whomever she wanted to talk with. Phone connections would not happen immediately and Lear dialed each number on the telephone using the rotary dial, which allowed the signal to be transmitted to the telephone number desired in an exchange. This was just the beginning of the telephone evolution as house phones no longer required a cord to be attached to the wall as they are now cordless, have multiple headsets, have speaker phones, three way calling capability, caller identification that can be connected to the television, and even speaks to Lear stating the name of the person calling as soon as the phone rings.

Symoné purchased a cell phone for Lear so that she could check in with her as she was out and about during the day. Even with prompting and role modeling, Lear continued to struggle with understanding how a phone can be used without being attached to a wall, how you did not hear a dial tone when you picked up the phone, that in order to send calls a specific button needed to be pushed, and how a cell phone can be used for multiple other reasons such as GPS, internet searches, watching shows and movies, and checking emails. With time, Lear was able to make phone calls using her flip cell phone, although this use was short lived.

There was no such thing as a computer until 1975, when the first personal computer was invented followed by the 5.25" floppy drive a year later to save additional documents that may have been too large for the computer's hard drive. Lear was not familiar with computers, how they operate or what they could be used for until more recently as computers are used in various facets of her life. For instance, typically every few months Lear goes to get lab work completed and checks in with the receptionist when she arrives. Most recently, Lear went to her usual lab office to have her routine lab work and was asked to check in using a computerized system which baffled her. There was a kiosk in the office where Lear was responsible for putting her first and last name in the system, scanning her insurance card, and answering a few questions. This is just another instance of the impact of technology has on the older generations.

Chapter Nine

While watching the news, Lear reflected on her first voting experience in 1948 in North Philadelphia near 8th and Poplar Streets with the registration process being a blur to her. This was the presidential election between democratic candidate Harry S. Truman and republican candidate Thomas E. Dewey. Truman was running for his second term as president and clearly demonstrated his support of liberal programs and the civil rights of African Americans. Lear had no concrete understanding of political parties and voted based on the assumption that the democrats were for the poor people and the republicans were for the rich. There were committees already in place who researched each candidate, then lobbied for the candidate they believed would best serve the public's interest. Lear utilized these individuals to inform her and then voted accordingly.

Although Lear did not closely follow political elections, she did not think about missing a voting opportunity as she learned that the voting experience was her way of having a voice in the implementation of laws and having some kind of legislative representation. She never had the experience of working at the polls on election day or even knew how the selection process worked but remembers that during her first encounters with voting there were more white people campaigning by ringing doorbells and handing out paper materials than anything else. People were not as interested in following political candidates back then and it was not common conversation like it is now. Lear would hear about the election on television then head to the voting polls on the designated day then watch the news later that evening to see who won. She does not remember anyone down South voting or even mentioning voting. This is possibly due to a minuscule number of African Americans even being registered to vote due to fear, discrimination, and literacy tests being consistent barriers. A version of this test would often be given to those who could not show proof of an elementary education, which was clearly created to discriminate against African Americans who often did not have the formal education due to lack of resources and ongoing poverty. It was not until 1965 that the Voting Rights Act was signed by President Johnson. This was a pivotal moment of change within the civil rights movement as the Voting Rights Act prohibited discrimination practices related to voting including, but not limited to, literacy tests.

Over 40 years later in 2008, a Democratic candidate and Illinois Senator Barack Obama and Republican candidate former House of Representatives member and then Senator John McCain ran against each other for the office of the President of the United States of America. Obama was a first time senator and McCain was looking to be the oldest president in history at 72 years old. Obama ran his campaign with the slogan "Change we can believe in" and the chant "Yes We

Can," focusing on instilling hope back into the American people during the recession where housing prices started to fall and the stock market crashed. Although Obama did not have a comparable amount of formal political experience, he quickly became what some would call America's favorite with his campaign focusing on healthcare and the economy. Although underestimated, Obama won the presidential election, making him the first African American and 44th President of the United States of America.

Lear initially did not think anything about President Obama running outside of him being black as this drew the interest of the public. Lear knew Jesse Jackson ran for president years prior but he did not come as close to winning as Obama. Lear paid more attention to Obama's campaign and wanted to vote for Obama partly because he was black but more so because he had a good reputation. Lear held onto the hope that he would win because he had as much "white people on his side as he did blacks," so he was able to win the election. Lear was ecstatic about President Obama's victory. It meant so much for her to see a black president with an educated wife and to watch others look up to him, showing younger generations that representation matters.

It never crossed Lear's mind that a black man would not only run for president with a realistic chance of winning but would in fact win the election. Lear watched the news and knew how many people were against him partly due to the color of his skin, so she prayed for him as a person and for his success in such a position of power knowing that everything he did would be scrutinized from him allegedly being a Muslim because of his middle name being Hussein, to the color suit he wore during press conferences, and even questioning his American citizenship but that did not have a noticeable impact on Obama as he continued to strive to help the working people. Obama always presented to the public as cool, calm, and collected in spite of all the targets on his back.

After four successful years in the most esteemed position in the country, President Obama ran for a second term as president in 2012 against Republican governor of Massachusetts, Mitt Romney. President Obama continued to campaign with his same platform focused on the economy. President Obama won the election with over 300 electoral votes where he only needed 270 to win. Lear was thoroughly excited to have President Obama represent the country for another four years. She continued to support him as a candidate because he was relatable, being raised by a single mother and often living with his maternal grandparents in a middle class home. Lear found President Obama to be confident but humble, well educated, intriguing, and more in touch with the average American than any other presidential candidate she had seen prior. Watching him on television became more common to Lear as she became more and more interested in the fate of the country and how the proposals President Obama made could directly impact her. To Lear, President Obama showed himself as being worth her vote with his strategies to improve the healthcare system for those uninsured and underinsured and developed with the help of the Senate and the House of Representatives, the Patient Protection and Affordable Care Act.

Although Lear favored President Obama, some news channels continued to speak about how he had hurt the economy and so forth. In spite of all the backlash President Obama received, Lear was internally satisfied knowing that he was the first African American elected and served as president for two consecutive terms while maintaining a remarkable public image with no scandals and worked towards improving life for those in poverty and the working American instead of giving tax breaks for the most wealthy of Americans. Lear acknowledges that President Obama may not have made all the "right" decisions but also acknowledges that he paved the way for the next African American candidate to run for presidency and for young African American children to know that it is possible to become the president of the United States of America, coming from a humble background with the secret to success being hard work.

Chapter Ten

Over the years, Lear had minor health issues but nothing that required surgery as she prided herself on staying active and eating a balanced diet. At eighty-four years old, Lear was told she had congestive heart failure. Of course, Lear knew that the heart, or as she calls it her "ticker," is a vital organ and that without it she cannot live. Congestive heart failure occurs when the heart cannot pump blood properly due to fluid build up. It was decided by the cardiology team at the local hospital that Lear would need an implantable cardioverter defibrillator (ICD) or often known as a defibrillator which is a small electronic device that is placed in a person's chest. This device is used to monitor the individual's heartbeat and in the event the heartbeat is slower, the device is used when the heart beats faster than expected or at an irregular rate. The device is designed to correct the rate in which the heart beats to prevent sudden death.

After multiple consults with cardiology and prayer, Lear decided to move forward with the surgery to improve her overall quality of life. Prior to the surgery, Symoné and Mary were right by Lear's side asking questions and praying for the surgery to go well. To no surprise, Lear stayed a very brief time in the hospital and went home with minor restrictions such as no lifting her arms above her head for a certain amount of time and to not lift heavy objects as she began to heal. After the surgery, Lear, Symoné, and Mary were told that recovery would take approximately four to six weeks so Symoné continued to live with Lear, helping her in whatever capacity she could and Mary came and stayed the night more often.

When it was time for the routine follow up appointment, the cardiology team noted that Lear was recovering at an impressive rate so she was able to resume all activities as normal. It was also mentioned that since the defibrillator was a machine, it would need to be replaced at a time that could not be determined but the team would continue to monitor the defibrillator's effectiveness. Lear was scheduled to follow up with cardiology every few months to check the rhythm of her heart rate and see how much longer the machine had to run and when a replacement could be expected.

After the initial surgery, Lear was provided with a machine that needed to be connected to the house telephone line and was used to transmit signals from the machine to the cardiology office where the physician could determine her progress or lack thereof every three months or so. Lear would be provided a date in which she was responsible to electronically transmit to the office and asked Symoné to assist. This would be done by Lear placing a small piece on her chest over the defibrillator while the machine that was connected to the phone line transmitted the signal sounding like a computer trying to connect to the internet. This entire process took 10-15 minutes and then the office would call Lear within a day or so if there were any issues. The home monitoring and office visits alternated every few months.

One day while at home doing routine housework, Lear heard a beeping noise. First she attributed the noise to the alarm as she was opening the door throwing out the trash but then she realized it was not the alarm as she continued to hear the beeping. Little did Lear know, the beeping noise she was hearing was her defibrillator letting her know it was time for a battery change. In 2010, after another consultation, Lear was again preparing for surgery. Symoné was spending the summer at college taking two courses so leaving at such a pivotal time was difficult. Since Symoné was away at college, Mary spent the night with Lear helping her with day to day tasks like getting dressed and food preparation. Symoné worried and prayed but tried to stay focused on school, managing to come home on the weekend only to find Lear in great condition wondering what the worrying was all about since she was doing fine. Once again, Lear had a speedy recovery with no concerns.

On a Sunday in October 2018, Symoné decided to stay home from church and rest but she was not prepared for what would happen that day. While laying in bed, Symoné received a call from Lear who was panting for breath saying she needed to go to the hospital because she could not breathe. Symoné attempted to triage the situation but told Lear she was on her way and would call her niece down the street to come down and further assess what was going on in the interim. As Symoné jumped out of bed to get dressed as quickly as she could, she called her niece who answered the phone and agreed to go down the street to check on Lear. As Symoné got into the car with her husband, she checked in with her niece who was concerned about Lear's breathing and told Symoné that she did not want an ambulance to be called but instead wanted Symoné to take her to the hospital. Although against Lear's wishes, Symoné instructed her niece to monitor Lear closely and if she got any worse to call the ambulance even if Lear objected to ensure she was safe.

As Symoné drove she prayed and made it to Lear's home in about twenty minutes parking in the middle of the street. When she walked in the door, Lear was sitting in her recliner still panting and having difficulty putting on her socks and shoes. Symoné put on Lear's socks, shoes, and jacket, then her husband helped Lear get up and walk out of the home to the car. Symoné went into the kitchen to double check the stove, grabbed Lear's medication then her wallet, and turned off all the lights as she locked the front door. She then drove to the nearest emergency room where Lear had been seen previously for cardiology support. Symoné dropped her husband and Lear off at the emergency room entrance while finding parking then calling and texting Mary to let her know that Lear needed to go to the emergency room.

Symoné helped Lear check in at the hospital where tests were completed and it was determined that Lear was retaining fluid related to her congestive heart failure, resulting in her being admitted for two days. Due to Lear's breathing restrictions, she was placed on oxygen while waiting to be taken to her room but remained able to talk to the medical team about what was going on with her, including sharing that she had been having trouble with her basic breathing for some time as she needed to take breaks when walking down the street but did not pay it any attention nor did she report this to Symoné. While out telling her husband about Lear's condition, Symoné made phone calls at Lear's request to her friends who would be expecting to talk to Lear that evening. The phone calls consisted of telling her friends which hospital she was at, that she would be admitted, and that Symoné would provide additional updates as they became available.

Shortly after Lear was officially admitted and taken to her room, Mary came to check on Lear, so Symoné went to grab food and made more phone calls to a few of Lear's family members in South Carolina who would in turn share that information with their other family members. Lear, Mary, and Symoné listened to the doctor's report and course of treatment, then Lear kicked Mary and Symoné out of her room saying they could go now because she was okay. They both laughed and said to themselves that Lear was okay since she was being sassy again. Symoné checked in with the nursing staff, and then her and Mary went home for the night.

Lear remained in the hospital for two days with the medical staff thinking she would need to go home on oxygen due to her oxygen level being high which Lear did not want. Much to their surprise, Lear made a full recovery and was ready to go home after those two days. Lear's attending physician called Symoné, who was at work at the time, describing how well Lear was doing and that she was going to be discharged. Symoné asked for a discharge time and was told it may take a couple hours to get all the paperwork together so she wrapped up things at work, called Mary to update her, and headed to the hospital to pick Lear up. When Symoné walked into Lear's room she was fully dressed and talking to her roommate in an upbeat and excited tone. As Lear said goodbye to her roommate, she walked out of the hospital perky with joy as she was heading home.

A few weeks later, Lear went to her cardiologist for a follow up appointment and learned that her current defibrillator was nearing its replacement time, therefore their recommendation would be another surgery for Lear at the age of ninety-five. Lear previously stated she did not want surgery again so Symoné thought her answer would be no to the surgery, but after much contemplation and months of consultations, Lear decided to proceed with the surgery and leave the rest up to God. While meeting with the cardiologist and nurse practitioner, Lear made her final decision to have the surgery and scheduled it for Wednesday, February 13, 2019. It was at that point that Symoné devised a plan including taking off work for at least two days, including the day of the surgery and the day after, along with preparing to spend the night with Lear following her return home. The week prior to the scheduled surgery, Lear went to have blood work completed and Lear's cousin who she raised as a child came from South Carolina to stay with her after the surgery.

The day of the surgery, Symoné received a phone call from Lear's niece asking if she was awake and Symoné reassured her that she was wide awake heading to pick up Lear. Lear's niece sounded relieved and asked for updates about the surgery as they became available. Symoné arrived to Lear's home early in the morning, picked her and her cousin up, and headed to the hospital. Symoné dropped Lear and her cousin off at the front door then parked the car. Once Symoné walked into the hospital, the three of them headed to the designated department for outpatient surgery where Lear was checked in and patiently waited for her 9am surgery. Hours passed and Lear was told that her surgeon was behind schedule as he was performing another surgery. While waiting, Lear's family and friends called Symoné asking for updates, but there were none. Symoné told everyone that once there were updates that she would share them.

At around 2pm, Lear finally went back to prep for surgery asking the hospital staff if Symoné could come back with her. The staff asked Lear if she was able to change on her own, which she confirmed she could, then they told her that once she was all set up for surgery that Symoné would be able to come back. Before Lear was taken to the operating room, Symoné and Lear's cousin were able to go back and see her. Once Lear saw Symoné, she shared that the staff wanted her to sign some paperwork but she would not do so without Symoné being present. It turned out that the paperwork Lear was referring to was the anesthesiologist who needed consent from Lear to give her anesthesia to numb her body and prevent her from feeling pain during surgery. Once all the paperwork was reviewed again, Symoné told Lear that the medicine was needed so she would not feel the pain as the surgeon made the incision, so Lear agreed to sign consent.

Symoné and Lear's cousin met with her and prayed for God to touch each person in the operating room from the surgeon to the nurses and the orderly staff. After leaving Lear, Symoné and Lear's cousin went to the cafeteria to grab lunch since they had not eaten all day. Within an hour or so of returning, Symoné checked in with the receptionist who confirmed that Lear was still in surgery. Since the surgery was expected to take roughly 45 minutes, Symoné sat down waiting for the physician to give an update afterwards. Symoné waited and waited, watching the doors as physicians came out to speak to other families but no one came to Symoné, who checked the television board that continued to state that Lear was in surgery. After a while, Lear's name was removed from the surgery list but still no one came out. By this time, Mary had come to the hospital asking how Lear was doing and all Symoné could do was pray..."If I have the faith, God has the power."

Finally the receptionist said Green was out of surgery and Symoné was finally able to exhale with relief. When it was confirmed that family could go back and see Lear, Symoné leaped at the chance. When she saw Lear's smiling face, she was so relieved that she could not contain her joy and began to stumble. Symoné began to thank God for allowing the surgery to go well and could not do anything but smile and kiss her Godmother. Once the initial response was over, Lear proceeded to tell Symoné that she could go home that night. Symoné was in shock but after talking to the doctor it was determined that Lear's surgery was a success and there was nothing that could be done in the hospital that could not be done at home. The medical staff took Lear's vitals learning that her blood pressure was elevated possibly due to her not taking medication that morning in preparation for surgery. Of course, the medical staff gave Lear medications and monitored her hoping that her blood pressure would go down. Symoné kissed Lear and told her that she would go outside and make phone calls to her family and friends with updates as Mary and Lear's cousin would also come back and visit with her.

As Mary and Lear's cousin took turns visiting her, the nurses tried to explain how to use the new defibrillator home monitoring system. Lear said, "My goddaughter needs to hear this" resulting in Lear's cousin and Mary coming to the waiting room to get Symoné. Symoné watched the nurses demonstrate how to use the monitoring device as Lear mentioned to her that she did not eat all day and stated that she was hungry. Symoné then asked the staff if there was something in the back that Lear could eat or if she could get her something from the cafeteria. Nursing staff came back with two cartons of juice and a roast beef sandwich. Symoné opened up the carton of orange juice and happily fed Lear the sandwich, smiling at her spunk and resilience. Within a couple hours, Symoné helped Lear get dressed being cautious of her chest area to not cause distress, then went to get the car. As Lear and her cousin approached the car, the hospital staff member complimented Lear on how well she looked for her age and Lear jumped in the car smiling as she was glad to go home.

Within a few days of being home, Lear wanted to move around and go back to her usual routine but was advised by Symoné to be careful not to overdo things because that could lead to complications. At her follow up visit with the head of cardiology at the hospital and the nurse practitioner, Lear was given what she would call "a clean bill of health" meaning she no longer had restrictions such as not lifting her arms above her head and her incision wound was healing quite impressively. Right after the follow up visit, Symoné took Lear and her cousin to the market at Lear's request as this was her first time out since the surgery. It was a sense of relief for Symoné knowing that Lear was healing properly aside from some swelling and she was also ready to resume her regular activities.

Chapter Eleven

In preparation for Lear's 95th birthday, Symoné wondered what she would do to celebrate. Since Symoné and Mary's family were going on a family cruise to the Bahamas with nearly fifteen people they thought to invite Lear to join their family and have a relaxing vacation. After several offers, Lear held her ground and declined to attend the cruise therefore Symoné began her search for a banquet hall to celebrate her birthday. This was a complex journey as Symoné wanted to have a spacious, clean, and handicap accessible banquet hall that had parking but knew that alcohol would not be provided, which some facilities try to sell. Since Lear was an excellent cook she was also particular about food when she went out, so Symoné knew she had to find a venue that would allow their guests to bring in their own food which would allow Symoné and Mary to do all the cooking to ensure that Lear was pleased.

After weeks of exploring options and pricing, Symoné found the perfect banquet hall located inside a church on a main street with two parking lots, one on each side with approximately thirty parking spots plus street parking. Symoné recruited Mary, emphasizing the significant milestone Lear was crossing and that it deserved to be celebrated. Five years prior, Symoné planned a surprise birthday party for Lear at The Pub in New Jersey inviting fifty people, including her cousin from South Carolina. This time around Symoné wanted a different location and at Mary's request, she asked Lear for her guestlist for the party to prevent anyone being left out. Lear provided the guestlist and Symoné did not supply her with any other details besides coordinating her outfit: a navy blue two piece gown with three quarter sleeves and sequin and lace at the top and silver glitter shoes with a small heel. Symoné knew Lear and that she liked to have control but also wanted Lear to trust her judgement and be surprised.

After months of preparing, the big day had arrived and Symoné was ready for Lear's party. Lear was brought to the party by one of her cousins and as she walked in smiling, she was greeted by her friends, family, and a professional photographer. At one entrance, Lear looked to her right and saw a trifold board with nearly a hundred pictures of herself throughout her lifetime with a gold and white guest book. Immediately she asked Symoné where did she get all the pictures from and Symoné laughed saying she took pictures with her phone of all Lear's pictures as they reminisced weeks prior. As Lear continued to walk into the hall, there were four rectangular tables on each side filled with her family and friends with clear centerpieces and gold, black, and white flowers with balloons to match floating high in the air. Each place setting was decorated to perfection with a square dinner plate and dessert plate trimmed in gold along with gold silverware and napkins.

As Symoné hugged Lear asking if she liked everything, she reminded Lear that she knew Lear well and would not do anything but the best for her, which is why she wanted Lear to trust her judgement. Symoné and Mary created an amazing experience for Lear with appetizers ranging from turkey meatballs, seafood salad, a fruit tray and a vegetable table followed by a sit down dinner which consisted of fried chicken, roast beef and gravy, baked macaroni and cheese, string beans, and a dinner roll. Lastly there was a dessert table filled with chocolate covered strawberries, pineapple coconut cake, cheesecake bites, cupcakes, and banana pudding.

Towards the end of the celebration, there was an opportunity for the guests to say a few words about Lear to everyone. As Mary stood to talk about Lear, she began describing their relationship and how influential Lear had been in her life and the lives of her children. Immediately following Mary, Symoné stood up and began speaking about her godmother and before she knew it, she was crying. As the words came out of her mouth all Symoné could think about was how much Lear had done for her over the years and how it could never be repaid resulting in nothing but tears of gratitude. Just as she cried, Lear did too. Symoné also presented Lear with a citation from two senators, one from another county and one from Philadelphia, acknowledging her 95th birthday. Lear cried more as the citation was read and Symoné knew her mission was accomplished as these were joys of joy. Some people say blood is thicker than water, referring to family being more important that friends, and Symoné can understand that but as far as she is concerned there is no biological relationship that could be stronger than that of her and her godmother.

* * *

What does life look like for Lear here and now? Lear continues to be a force to be reckoned with as she lives independently, handling all her basic necessities from bathing, cooking for herself and others, cleaning her 3 bedroom 1.5 bathroom home to perfection, to catching public transportation throughout the city, to running her day to day errands at 95 years old. Lear, at times, gets on a ladder to paint the inside of her home and the lower extremities of the outside of her home as she sees fit. When asked by Symoné to help her, Lear clearly stated, "There will be a time I cannot do for myself then you can help me, but until then let me do it." Although Symoné wants to help, out of respect she acknowledges Lear's desire to maintain her independence and honors her wishes. Lear continues to spend time with her Cornerstone church family going to Sunday church services, revivals, dinners, and overall fellowship as these people are near and dear to her heart. Lear embraces her age and uses any opportunity to tell people whether on the bus or in the supermarket how old she is, only to hear their shocking response of how good she looks for her age while asking how she has gotten to live so long.

During reflection, Lear thinks about education and how she would have continued going to school if she would have known how important it was when she was younger. Lear sacrificed her education to help her family on the farm to prosper but wonders how life would have been if she would have gone further along in school. Lear finds it hard to believe that children these days have so much afforded to them, from the ability to go to school with ease and for free but still decides not to attend. She shares how poor she was and how children these days have everything handed to them and still do not listen to their parents. This leaves Lear in utter disbelief. Looking back over her life and everything she has been through, she describes her success as nothing but the grace of God who has allowed her to keep pressing forward during her darkest times, and now she does not want for anything. She has paid her debt to society so she can decide whether to go out and run errands or stay home and watch television all day, which she rarely does.

Symoné makes it her business to talk to Lear daily to check in on how she is doing and see if there is anything she needs. This call usually takes place after 9pm, which allows Lear time to run her errands and be back home to tell Symoné all about her day. Once in a while Symoné will call Lear after 9pm and she will not answer, so Symoné waits for a few minutes and calls back. It is at that time she calls her niece down the street from Lear to go to the house, ring the doorbell, and see if everything is alright before Symoné drives down to the house. One particular day Symoné called Lear and was greeted by her voicemail. After several tries Symoné asked her niece if she had seen Lear. Symoné's niece responded saying yes, she was outside earlier watering her plants on her porch. As Symoné's niece went outside to check on Lear, she saw Lear sitting on her front porch watching the neighborhood people's interactions and enjoying the summer breeze.

As Symoné's niece was greeted by Lear, Symoné asked to speak to Lear. Symoné proceeded to ask Lear what she was doing outside at this time of night and told Lear that she was getting worried. Lear calmly asked Symoné what time it was for Symoné to reply

Symoné Miller

nine something. Lear then told Symoné that she should
not worry about Lear until after 10pm. Symoné laughed
as she knew Lear was okay because her response
remained as sassy as ever.

There were other incidents where Symoné would
repeatedly call Lear only to get her voicemail so
Symoné would begin calling her close friends from
church to see if Lear was supposed to attend a function
in the evening. If Lear's close friend did not know
where she was, Symoné and the friend would begin
calling around to other friends in the hope of figuring
out where Lear was. After all the calls, it was always
determined that Lear was safe and sound spending
quality time in the company of her friends. As Lear
began to see how concerned Symoné was, she would
either call Symoné before going out in the evening or
she would tell Symoné about the event the day prior.
There was a mutual level of respect between Lear and
Symoné. Lear knew how much Symoné cared for her
and how wicked people in the world could be,
especially to those who may have been seen as
vulnerable due to their age.

In a way Lear states she lived a good life because
some people say they want to be like Lear one day. She
states she must have a good streak somewhere if people
say they want to be like her. Symoné asked Lear what
she would like to leave behind for the world to know
about her. Lear's response was to follow her footsteps
and what she did in life. Lear's advice for the upcoming
generations is to stay in school and work for what you
want. Lear did not learn about money but feels the
value of money was ingrained in her. As a child, people
did not have much money to give her so they would
give her one to two pennies. Instead of going out and

spending every cent she made, Lear would save her money. There was no particular reason she saved her money, she just did not have anything she needed or wanted, which is a lesson in delaying self-gratification and sacrificing for the long-term goals even if they have not been set yet.

Lear worked for decades and did not even describe it as working hard then because she was doing what she needed to do, so she wants to remind the younger people to remain steadfast and work hard even when no one around you is doing so or understands your rationale because it will pay off in the long run. One request Lear had made for those reading this book is to challenge yourself and change your ways related to hate and to learn how to love and forgive people as angering quickly will not get you anywhere in life. During a conversation with Symoné, Lear was asked, how did you get to be 95 years old? Lear responded: "Live right, get your proper rest but in the end it is all God's doing. It's none of my doing, only God's doing."

Lear's Red Rice Recipe

INGREDIENTS

1 cooking onion

1.5 pounds of rice

1-2 tablespoons of butter or margarine

1 can or 28 ounces of crushed tomatoes

1-2 tablespoons of sugar

Salt and pepper to taste

INSTRUCTIONS

1. Grate entire onion in pot and sauté with butter or margarine
2. Add crushed tomatoes and mix well with salt, pepper and sugar to taste
3. Once cooked add rice to sauce mixture
4. Cover rice and cook for approximately 15 minutes
5. Put rice covered with lid in the oven for another 15-30 minutes until fully cooked
6. ENJOY!!!!

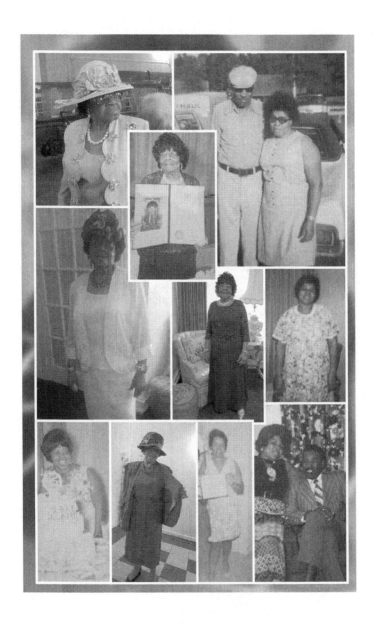

Discussion Questions

1. What would you consider successful aging in the 21st century?
2. What are some strengths and vulnerabilities within the biological, psychological, and social areas of Lear's life?
3. What are some ethical dilemmas that were raised throughout Lear's lifetime and how could they have been addressed?
4. What are some of Lear's protective factors?

Symoné Miller is a Licensed Clinical Social Worker (LCSW) who specializes in psychotherapy with adults and the geriatric population. She completed her Bachelor of Social Work at Bloomsburg University of Pennsylvania with a concentration in Children, Family, and Youth. She then received her Masters of Social Service at Bryn Mawr College Graduate School of Social Work and Social Research with the following focuses: Adult Development and Aging along with Children and Adolescents.

Symone' obtained a postgraduate certificate in Cognitive Behavioral Therapy in 2014. She is a member of the Pennsylvania Society for Clinical Social Work (PSCSW). She is also the owner and founder of Expanding Your Horizons, LLC that specializes in therapy and clinical supervision.

Symone' was born and raised in the City of Brotherly Love and Sisterly Affection, Philadelphia, where she resides with her husband.

Divine Legacy
PUBLISHING, LLC.

Creative Control With Self-Publishing

Divine Legacy Publishing provides authors with the guid-ance necessary to take creative control of their work through self-publishing. We provide:

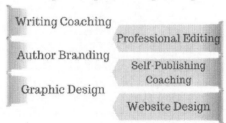

Writing Coaching

Professional Editing

Author Branding

Self-Publishing Coaching

Graphic Design

Website Design

Let Divine Legacy Publishing help you master the business of self-publishing.

Made in the
USA
Lexington, KY